WRIT-ING DEGREE ZERO

and

ELE-MENTS OF SEMI-OLOGY

WRIT-ING DEGREE ZERO

and

ELE-MENTS OF SEMI-OLOGY

Preface by Susan Sontag

Beacon Press
Boston

by Roland Barthes

Translated from the
French by Annette
Lavers and Colin Smith

Writing Degree Zero is translated from
   the French *Le Degré Zéro de L'Ecriture*
© 1953 by Editions du Seuil
Translation © 1967 by Jonathan Cape Ltd.
Preface copyright © 1968 by Susan Sontag

Elements of Semiology is translated from
   the French *Éléments de Sémiologie*
© 1964 by Editions du Seuil
Translation © 1967 by Jonathan Cape Ltd.

Library of Congress catalog card number: 75–105325
Standard Book Number: 8070–1545–8
First published as a Beacon Paperback in 1970
   by arrangement with Hill and Wang, Inc.

Beacon Press books are published under the auspices
   of the Unitarian Universalist Association
9   8   7   6   5   4   3   2

ELE-
MENTS
OF
SEMI-
OLOGY

WRIT-
ING
DEGREE
ZERO

Writing Degree Zero

Contents

PREFACE

To describe Barthes as a literary critic does him an obvious injustice. A man of prodigious learning, unflagging mental energy, and acutely original sensibility, he has established his credentials as aesthetician, literary and theatre critic, sociologist, metapsychologist, social critic, historian of ideas, and cultural journalist. Only if the ideal of criticism is enlarged to take in a wide variety of discourse, both theoretical and descriptive, about culture, language, and contemporary consciousness, can Barthes plausibly be called a critic. Karl Kraus, T. W. Adorno, and Kenneth Burke come to mind as other distinguished examples of this rare breed of intellectual virtuoso, while McLuhan suggests the risks of radical unevenness of quality and judgment incurred with this magnitude of intellectual appetite and ambition. Evaluation at this virtually unclassifiable level of achievement may seem somewhat frivolous. Still, I would argue that Barthes is the most consistently intelligent, important, and useful critic —stretching that term—to have emerged anywhere in the last fifteen years.

Writing Degree Zero, long overdue in English translation, is Barthes' first book; it appeared in 1953. Seen from the perspective of 1968, however, *Writing Degree Zero* probably isn't the easiest text with which to start an acquaintance with Barthes. The book is compact to the point of ellipsis, often arcane. It barely suggests the variety and intellectual mobility of Barthes' subsequent work — which now totals six books, only one of which has already been brought out in the United States,* and numerous uncollected essays. Though explicitly theoretical in character, the argument here can't compare in rigor or completeness with Barthes' later development of some of these ideas in his "Eléments de Sémiologie," the systematic treatise first published in issue No. 4 (1964) of *Communications*, the important French journal of which he is an editor. Moreover, *Writing Degree Zero* gives virtually no indication of Barthes' sensitivity and imaginativeness in handling individual literary texts and and in stating the unifying metaphors of a single author's body of work, skills he was to exercise in the short book on Michelet (1954) and in the influential studies of Brecht and Robbe-Grillet written in the mid 1950's. Lastly, the present text doesn't disclose the witty concreteness of Barthes' sensibility, his talent for sensuous phenomenological description, evidenced in the brilliant essay-epiphanies collected in 1957 under the title *Mythologies*. Thus, *Writing Degree Zero* is early Barthes, seminal but not representative. (Perhaps only the collection published in 1964, *Essais Critiques*, spanning work from 1953 to 1963, gives in one book anything like a reasonable sample of Barthes' range.) And, even apart from this proviso, the book may present considerable difficulties to the reader unacquainted with the background and provenance of Barthes' argument.

Sur Racine (1963) was published by Hill and Wang in 1964 as *On Racine*, in a translation by Richard Howard.

Writing Degree Zero must be located in the context of a cultural situation in two important respects unlike our own.

First, Barthes is addressing a literary community which has for several generations, on most levels, honored and treated as central a canon of contemporary work still regarded as marginal and suspect by the Anglo-American literary community. Such "difficult" literary tendencies as Symbolism and Surrealism, and in particular the line of post-novel prose narrative from the Surrealist fictions to those of Borges, Beckett, and Robbe-Grillet, are taken to occupy the central position in contemporary letters — while most novels in traditional "realistic" forms (such as continue to this day to be *critical* successes in England and America) are regarded as essentially uninteresting, barely noteworthy products of a retarded or reactionary consciousness. Inevitably, this triumph of literary "modernism" in Paris has had its impact on critical debate, shifting the substantive concerns and the tone of serious literary discussion. In this country, of course, a quite different taste prevails, and comparable work — from late Joyce, Stein, and late Virginia Woolf to Burroughs — is still generally regarded as a provocative minority current, labeled "avant-garde" or "experimental" literature. (The critical situation that *is* comparable here is the consensus of "avant-garde" standards for painting which have prevailed ever since the early 1950's, with the consecration by both the art-world elite and Time-Life style popularizers of Pollock, DeKooning, Kline, Motherwell, Rothko, *et al.*)

Second, Barthes' book is a late contribution to that vigorous debate that has engaged the European literary community since the decade before the war on the relation between politics and literature. No debate of similar quality on that topic ever took place here. Despite all rumors that there once existed a generation of politically radical writers in England and America, the question of the political-ethical responsibility of writers was never posed here in anything better than an embryonic, intellectually crude form—a lone exception being the brilliant books published in the late 1930's by the young Christopher Caudwell.

It's against this background that *Writing Degree Zero* must be situated. Because Barthes is addressing a sizable literary community at home in and respectful of literary modernism, most of which has accepted some variety of left-wing or neo-Marxist political stance—both conditions, especially the former, being quite untypical of the literary community in the English-speaking world—he simply takes for granted a great deal that we do not. *Writing Degree Zero* lends support to the already well-established cause of advanced literature, not with an argument over fundamentals of taste and purpose, but by an allusive refinement of that argument, oriented more to modernist literature's further prospects than to its celebrated past. But *Writing Degree Zero* is not only manifesto but polemic. With any difficult text, the reader, in order to understand what the philosopher or critic is arguing *for*, must grasp what or whom he is tacitly arguing *against*. Considered as a polemic, Barthes is challenging the most intelligent version of the theory of literature's obligation to be socially committed, that theory having always entailed some attack, overt or implicit, on the tradition of modernist literature.

Indeed, I think, one can name the specific adversary of Barthes' argument. Barthes' topic is the same as that posed by, and stated in the title of, Sartre's famous *What Is Literature?* (Supplementary confirmation by dates:

although *Writing Degree Zero* was published in 1953, early portions of it appeared in the newspaper *Combat* in 1947, the same year Sartre's book was published. And both Sartre's first chapter and the first section of *Writing Degree Zero* have the same title: ("What Is Writing?"). It would seem that Barthes, though he never mentions Sartre's book, had it in mind when he wrote *Writing Degree Zero*, and that his argument constitutes an attempt at refuting Sartre's. Where *What Is Literature?* is prolix (but easily readable) and contains extended passages of powerful, concrete historical and psychological analysis of the writer's situation and of postwar society, *Writing Degree Zero* is terse and unconcrete (and rather difficult of access)—as if Barthes were depending on his reader's familiarity with the generous development of the terms of the debate provided by Sartre.

Sartre takes the position, already advanced for different purposes by Valéry, that prose literature differs from all the other arts, by virtue of its means—language. Words, unlike images, signify; they convey meaning. Therefore, prose literature by its nature is bound, as is no other art, including poetry, to the task of communicating. The writer is (potentially) a giver of consciousness, a liberator. His medium, language, confers on him an ethical obligation: to aid in the project of bringing liberty to *all* men—and this ethical criterion must be the foundation of any sound literary judgment. Thus Sartre's inquiry into the nature of literature is throughout governed by this ethical conception of the writer's vocation, as is his relatively pejorative treatment of the "crisis of language which broke out at the beginning of this century," which he characterizes as a situation favoring the production of private, obscurantist literary art works confined to "an audience of specialists." Believing that "literature is in essence a taking of positions," Sartre argues that "art has never been on the side of the purists."

Disregarding much of the feast of argument in Sartre's brilliant book, Barthes' thesis in *Writing Degree Zero* confronts only this basic view of literature by which Sartre supports his theory of the writer's "engagement." Sartre begins by distinguishing *language,* whose "end" or function is to communicate, from *style,* understood as the most efficient means of expressing the "subject," of putting down something. Language is the collective inventory, what is given to the writer; style is what is chosen, the "how" one renders "what one wants to write about." In refutation, Barthes offers a subtler set of categories. Instead of the common-sense dualism of language (social property) and style (individual decision), Barthes proposes the triad of language, style, and "writing." (These he calls the three dimensions of "form." Compare Sartre's astonishingly naive statement: "There is nothing to be said about form in advance, and we have said nothing. Everyone invents his own, and one judges it afterward.")

Thus Barthes begins with an account of language, one in essential agreement with Sartre's. Language, whose function is communication, is both "a social object" and "a kind of natural ambiance," the writer's "horizon," his "field of action," something that "enfolds the whole of literary creation" without endowing it with any specific form or content. All of history stands behind language — history "unified and complete in the manner of a natural order." Barthes was to adopt a different and far more complex view of language in later books — when he came under the successive influence of Saussurian linguistics, then of the ahistorical methods of "structural" analysis developed by Jakobson and Lévi-Strauss, and, most recently, of the account of the relation of language and the unconscious expounded by Lacan. But in this first book, it is only when Barthes treats the second of Sartre's pair of terms, style, that the difference made by having added a third term shows up.

By style Barthes means something quite different from the servant of content (as Sartre would have it). Its frame of reference is not historical, like language's, but "biological or biographical." Style is "indifferent to society," a closed "personal process." In its origin "the transmutation of a humour," style "is never anything but metaphor." Therefore, in Barthes' conceptual geography, style resides "outside art" (since it is "outside the pact that binds the writer to society") just as much as language does. If language stands on the "hither side of literature," style is located beyond it.

What remains for Barthes is the task of identifying what is peculiar to (or inside) literature, something that has to be distinct from both language and style. For this third term Barthes uses *écriture*, which may cause English-language readers difficulty. To translate *écriture* as "writing" is literally correct, but Barthes' meaning relies on a special inflection of the French word that has no equivalent in the English "writing." (Once we had the word "scripture," but that's no longer available.) A more helpful translation of what Barthes means by *écriture* — the ensemble of features of a literary work such as tone, ethos, rhythm of delivery, naturalness of expression, atmosphere of happiness or malaise — might be "personal utterance." For Barthes a language and a style are "objects," while a mode of *écriture* (writing, personal utterance) is a "function." Neither strictly historical nor irredeemably personal, *écriture* occupies a middle ground; it is "essentially the morality of form." In contrast to a language and a style, *écriture* is the writer's zone of freedom, "form considered as human intention."

It should be evident that Barthes' reply to Sartre hardly reasserts a doctrine of literature for literature's sake. Barthes isn't claiming that literature does or should exist in a social, historical, or ethical vacuum. As Barthes says, every given mode of *écriture* owes its existence to "the writer's consideration of the social use which he has chosen for his form and his committment to this choice." But literature, conceived as an instrumentality, cannot be confined to its social or ethical context. Insisting on the implications of Sartre's Kantian conception of the writer as the guardian of ideal "ends," Barthes suggests that Sartre has suppressed the fact that the choices made by writers always face in *two* directions: toward society and toward the nature of literature itself. Though the choice of a given manner of *écriture* amounts to "the choice of that social area within which the writer elects to situate the nature of his language," the writer can't place literature at the service of a social group or ethical end (as Sartre implies), deciding matters of "actual consumption." The writer's choice—which amounts to "a way of conceiving literature"—is a matter of "conscience, not of efficacy."

What Barthes is trying to allow is a more complex view of literature—a view of literature freed from the simplifications imposed by yielding to ethical euphoria, innocent of the necessity of "judgment." In many ways, of course, Barthes is close to Sartre's ethical and political position of that time—the values of "freedom," the contempt for the impasses of bourgeois culture, the horizon of the Revolution. What most profoundly separates them is their capacity for the moralistic judgment, so that Barthes can go a certain way with all of Sartre's

arguments but must stop well short of their final crystal-
lization—as when Sartre suggests that modernist literature (with its accelerating fragmentation of personal
utterance) embodies the final cop-out of "bourgeois
consciousness," a default which can be reversed only by
the ascendancy of a new, "revolutionary consciousness."
Barthes at that time was perfectly capable of using this
fairly crude left-Hegelian rhetoric—a good part of the
later argument of his book relies on the distinction between "classical language" and "bourgeois language"—
and would have agreed, probably still agrees, with most
of the ingredients that enter into this diagnosis, such as
the view that literature is passing through the most profound and desperate crisis of its language and means.
Still, Barthes could never end with so flat a judgment.
For instance, he is disinclined to attribute bad faith or
moral delinquency to the great writers from Flaubert
forward who have erected literature into a fundamentally
problematic activity. (Indeed, as he points out, it's only
recently that literature, strictly speaking, comes into
existence—as a problem.) Further, Barthes is skeptical—
rightly, I think—of the solution Sartre envisages. As he
says, "There is no writing which can be lastingly revolutionary." (Scathing judgment *is* reserved—this is 1953
—about the way most Communist writers employ a
language steeped in conventionality, presenting "reality
in a prejudged form" and thereby perpetuating "a bourgeois writing which bourgeois writers have themselves
condemned long ago." Barthes remarks that the writing
typical of all authoritarian regimes always seeks to pro-
mote "order," i.e. repression.)

Thus, while Barthes' austere, aphoristic book lacks
anything comparable to the eloquence and noble passion
of the long passages of moral exhortation in *What Is*

Literature? (particularly the chapter "Why Write?"), it should be remembered with what simplifications of the issue Sartre has paid for the ethical elevation of his argument. Barthes, though far from refusing the ethical dimension of Sartre's argument, shows that these matters are much more complex than Sartre conceived them. As Barthes says, *écriture* is always "an ambiguous reality: on the one hand, it unquestionably arises from a confrontation of the writer with the society of his time; on the other hand, from this social finality, it refers the writer back, by a sort of tragic reversal, to the sources, that is to say, the instruments of creation."

I have done little more than describe some leading themes of *Writing Degree Zero*. But because of the danger that Barthes' argument will itself be simplified, readers should be warned against being misled by the book's title. That title suggests a rather single-minded manifesto, advocating a stern retrenchment of literature into a desiccated, ascetic noncommunicativeness. This suggestion is likely to be reinforced for those readers aware that Barthes first became well known in France when he emerged as Robbe-Grillet's most eloquent spokesman — notably in three essays, "Le monde-objet" (1953), "Littérature objective" (1954), and "Littérature littérale" (1955), all included in *Essais Critiques* — in which he championed the ingenious and strategic reduction of literary means (i.e. of *style* as Barthes here uses the word) achieved by Robbe-Grillet by de-anthropomorphizing, eliminating metaphor, etc. But it would be a mistake to read *Writing Degree Zero* merely or even mainly as a polemic preparing the way for the advent of the "solution" of Robbe-Grillet. Actually the notion of zero-degree, neutral, colorless writing — first discussed by Sartre, who called it *l'écriture blanche*, in his famous review of Camus' *L'Etranger*—enters Barthes' argument only briefly: in the introduction (pp. 4–5), as the "last episode of a Passion of writing, which recounts stage by stage the disintegration of bourgeois consciousness," and again at the end (pp. 76–78) as *one* solution to the disintegration of literary language.

But this horizon of literature's final solution is only a boundary-concept, generated by this argument. It is the logical extension of the type of rhetoric Barthes uses. But it is the ground rules of that rhetoric which should be of much more interest and importance to the reader—and have been to Barthes himself, judging from the minor role that the notion of zero-degree writing has played in his subsequent literary studies. What is essential to Barthes' position is not its apocalyptic terminus, but the diagnosis of the over-all situation of literature he makes. Barthes views that peculiarly modern phenomenon of "the multiplication of modes of writing" as an inevitable development. As literature abolishes "more and more its condition as a bourgeois myth," *écriture* pushes aside language and style, absorbing "the whole identity of a literary work." Barthes affirms—and here his thinking strongly reflects the influence of Blanchot—the way literature verges on becoming a total experience, one which brooks no limits, and cannot be permanently stabilized or held in check by any particular strategy of writing, the adoption of zero-degree writing including. As modern literature is the history of alienated "writing" or personal utterance, literature aims inexorably at its own self-transcendence—at the abolition of literature. But Barthes' point would seem to be that no amount of moral exhortation or conceptual unraveling is going to alter drastically this tense, paradoxical state of affairs. "In spite of the efforts made in our time, it has proved impossible successfully to liquidate literature entirely."

This would seem to leave the heaviest burden on the critic, who mediates amid competing chaos—a task Barthes has heroically exemplified in his own ambitious body of work. Thus, in *Writing Degree Zero*, Barthes presupposes both the effort of writers like Valéry, Joyce, Stein, Beckett, and Burroughs to abolish literature and the effort of other writers to confine literature to ethical communication (the notion of "engaged" writing). It is in this agonized suspension between the contradictory goals entertained by literature, I should argue, that the discourse of the responsible critic situates itself—without yielding to an easy dismissal of either position.

Of course, these efforts to liquidate literature have left their trace, which explains the tone, both hectic and detached, with which Barthes approaches his topic. At times, one could describe Barthes' stance in this book as almost an anthropological one, to the extent that he implies that all thinking both about and within literature operates by means of myths. Thus he speaks of the novel as a "mythological object," and of the "rituals" of literature.

The other prominent gesture by which he distances himself from his volatile subject is through constant recourse to a historical perspective. (This is more marked in Part Two of *Writing Degree Zero*, which connects with certain arguments in the latter part of Sartre's book on the historical situation of the contemporary writer, and on writing as a social institution.) But while Barthes shares with Sartre a familiar terminology, adapted from the Hegelian metahistorical scheme of consciousness, *Writing Degree Zero* lacks the detailed, concrete feeling for historical process in evidence in Sartre's book (particularly in the final chapter, "The Situation of the

Writer in 1947"). The history Barthes continually invokes always wears a capital H. This is perhaps the most serious limit to the argument of *Writing Degree Zero:* that, while insisting on a historical perspective, Barthes employs such a generalized, thin notion of history. Barthes is not so much referring to a real state of affairs as he is using a metaphor, which allows him to describe literature as a process rather than as a static entity. The particular value of history as an organizing myth is that it provides Barthes with a decisive moment, up to which the situation he describes leads and from which it proceeds — a paradigmatic "fall" of literature, which took place around 1850 and is best incarnated in the consciousness of Flaubert.

Most readers will probably find Part Two of *Writing Degree Zero* easier going than Part One, because even Barthes' pseudohistorical concreteness makes the argument somewhat less abstract, and more openly polemical. (Among the highly effective polemical passages is the attack on Socialist Realism in the section "Writing and Revolution.") But it's in Part One that the essentials of Barthes' view are laid out. Also, Part One suggests more of Barthes' later thinking, in particular his interest in consciousness conceived as an arena of classificatory schemes and systems. The maneuvers of consciousness, bracketed here by the rather simple notions of "myth" and "history," are elaborated in Barthes' later books in the light of Bachelardian phenomenology (*Michelet*) and Freudian psychology (*Sur Racine*), and, more recently, by approaches which are both ahistorical and apsychological: contemporary linguistics and the "structuralist" techniques of decoding and classification developed by Lévi-Strauss. The great advantage Barthes has gained from his new perspective is that anything can be subjected to the ahistorical, apsychological methods of structuralist analysis. A text does not mean only a literary text, as language is not the only "system of meaning." Thus, in recent years, Barthes has increasingly turned his attention to extra-linguistic languages.*

Barthes' vision of what thinking really is—an insatiable project, endlessly producing and consuming "systems," metaphor-haunted classifications of an ultimately opaque reality—receives only a very elementary exposure in *Writing Degree Zero*. In the present book, he appears at least as much the uncritical accomplice of myths as he is their classifier. Deploying some familiar creative fictions of contemporary intellectual life, such as the Hegelian "history of consciousness," the existentialist "freedom," the Marxist "bourgeois society," etc., Barthes proposes one new myth—that of *écriture*—for the purpose of analyzing a myth, that of "literature." Of course, "myth" doesn't mean that a concept (or argument or narrative) is false. Myths are not descriptions but rather models for description (or thinking)—according to the formula of Lévi-Strauss logical techniques for resolving basic antinomies in thought and social existence. And the converse is also true: all explanatory models for fundamental states of affairs, whether sophisticated or primitive, are myths. From this structuralist point of view, one can't object to *Writing Degree Zero* simply because its leading concepts are intellectual myths or fictions.

* Cf. the essays on Garbo's face, on wine, on detergents, on astrology, on costume, etc., in *Mythologies;* the studies, "La message photographique" in *Communications* No. 1 (1961) and "Rhétorique de l'image" in *Communications* No. 4 (1964), which deal mainly with advertising texts, to the recent big book, *Système de la Mode* (1967), which examines the classificatory systems implicit in women's clothing as reflected in the language used in fashion magazines.

What matters is that Barthes' myths about literature are extremely talented, even masterful, and do satisfy the need for intellectual cohesion (comparable to the way myths in the more ordinary sense, according to Lévi-Strauss, produce social cohesion).

After all, it isn't Barthes who made "literature" into a myth. He found it in that condition, along with all the other arts in our time. Someday perhaps a demystification of the myth of "art" (as an absolute activity) will be possible and will take place, but it seems far from that moment now. At this stage, only new myths can subdue —even for the brief time to permit contemplation—the old myths which move convulsively about us. Measured on this scale of need, the myths about literature proposed in *Writing Degree Zero* seem to me sturdy, subtle, and highly serviceable. They acknowledge basic antinomies that even the most gifted minds addressing the same subject, such as Sartre, have glossed over. And to anyone seriously caught up in the lacerating dialectics imposed by the stand of advanced art and consciousness in our time, the myths/models deployed by Barthes can also be recommended for their healing, therapeutic value.

SUSAN SONTAG

INTRODUCTION

Hébert, the revolutionary, never began a number of his news-sheet *Le Père Duchêne* without introducing a sprinkling of obscenities. These improprieties had no real meaning, but they had significance. In what way? In that they expressed a whole revolutionary situation. Now here is an example of a mode of writing* whose function is no longer only communication or expression, but the imposition of something beyond language, which is both History and the stand we take in it.

It is impossible to write without labelling oneself: as with *Le Père Duchêne*, so equally with Literature. It too must signify something other than its content and its individual form, something which defines its

* *Écriture*, which in French normally means only 'handwriting' or 'the art of writing', is now more and more frequently used as a substantive corresponding to all senses of the verb *écrire*, generally to mean the style, the fact of composing a work, or the actions which properly belong to a writer. It is used here in a strictly technical sense to denote a new concept, and is translated as 'writing', 'mode of writing'. This concept is discussed further in relation to that of 'idiolect' in *Elements of Semiology* (I.1.6 and I.1.7), as is that of 'zero degree'.

limits and imposes it as Literature. Whence a set of signs unrelated to the ideas, the language or the style, and setting out to give definition, within the body of every possible mode of expression, to the utter separateness of a ritual language. This hieratic quality of written Signs establishes Literature as an institution and clearly tends to place it above History, for no limits can be set without some idea of permanence. Now it is when History is denied that it is most unmistakably at work; it is therefore possible to trace a history of literary expression which is neither that of a particular language, nor that of the various styles, but simply that of the Signs of Literature, and we can expect that this purely formal history may manifest, in its far from obscure way, a link with the deeper levels of History.

We are naturally concerned with a link the form of which may well vary with History itself; there is no need to invoke direct determinism in order to feel that History underlies the fortunes of modes of writing: this kind of functional front, which sweeps along events, situations and ideas in the current of historical time, does not so much produce effects as set limits to choice. History, then, confronts the writer with a necessary option between several moral attitudes connected with language; it forces him to signify Literature in terms of possibilities outside his control. We shall see, for example, that the ideological unity of the bourgeoisie gave rise to a single mode of writing, and that in the bourgeois periods (classical and romantic), literary form could not be divided because consciousness was not; whereas, as soon as the writer ceased to be a witness to the universal, to become the incarnation of a tragic awareness (around 1850), his first gesture was to choose the commitment of his form, either by adopting or rejecting the writing of his past. Classical writing therefore disintegrated, and the whole of Literature, from Flaubert to the present day, became the problematics of language.

This was precisely the time when Literature (the word having come into being shortly before) was finally established as an object. Classical art could have no sense of being a language, for it *was* language, in other words it was transparent, it flowed and left no deposit, it brought ideally together a universal Spirit and a decorative sign without substance or responsibility; it was a language 'closed' by social and not natural bounds. It is a well-known fact that towards the end of the eighteenth century this transparency becomes clouded; literary form develops a second-order power independent of its economy and euphemistic charm; it fascinates the reader, it strikes him as exotic, it enthralls him, it acquires a weight. Literature is no longer felt as a socially privileged mode of transaction, but as a language having body and hidden depths, existing both as dream and menace.

This is important: literary form may henceforth elicit those existential feelings lying at the heart of any object: a sense of strangeness or familiarity, disgust or indulgence, utility or murder. For a century now, every mode of writing has thus been an exercise in reconciliation with, or aversion from, that objectified Form inevitably met by the writer on his way, and which he must scrutinize, challenge and accept with all its consequences, since he cannot ever destroy it without destroying himself as a writer. Form hovers before his gaze like an object; whatever he does, it is a scandal: if it stands resplendent, it appears outmoded; if it is a law unto itself, it is asocial; in so far as it is particular in relation to time or mankind, it cannot but mean solitude.

The whole nineteenth century witnessed the progress of this dramatic phenomenon of concretion. In Chateaubriand it is still only a trace, a light pressure of linguistic euphoria, a kind of narcissism in which the manner of writing is scarcely separable from its instrumental function and merely mirrors itself. Flaubert – to take only the typical stages of this process – finally established Literature as an object, through promoting literary labour to the status of a value; form became the end-product of craftsmanship, like a piece of pottery or a jewel (one must understand that craftsmanship was here made manifest, that is, it was for the first time imposed on the reader as a spectacle). Mallarmé's work, finally, was the crowning achievement of this creation of Literature as Object, and this by the ultimate of all objectifying acts: murder. For we know that the whole effort of Mallarmé was exerted towards the destruction of language, with Literature reduced, so to speak, to being its carcass.

From an initial non-existence in which thought, by a happy miracle, seemed to stand out against the backcloth of words, writing thus passed through all the stages of a progressive solidification; it was first the object of a gaze, then of creative action, finally of murder, and has reached in our time a last metamorphosis, absence: in those neutral modes of writing, called here 'the zero degree of writing', we can easily discern a negative momentum, and an inability to maintain it within time's flow, as if Literature, having tended for a hundred years now to transmute its surface into a form with no antecedents, could no longer find purity anywhere but in the absence of all signs, finally proposing the realization of this Orphean dream: a writer without Literature. Colourless writing like Camus's, Blanchot's or Cayrol's, for example, or conversational writing like Queneau's, represents the last episode of a Passion of writing, which recounts stage by stage the disintegration of bourgeois consciousness.

What we hope to do here is to sketch this connection; to affirm the existence of a formal reality independent of language and style; to try to show

that this third dimension of Form equally, and not
without an additional tragic implication, binds the
writer to his society; finally to convey the fact that
there is no Literature without an Ethic of language.
The limited length of this essay (a few pages of which
appeared in 1947 and 1950 in *Combat*) is sufficient
indication that what is offered here is no more than
an Introduction to what a History of Writing might
be.

Part One

WHAT IS WRITING?

We know that a language is a corpus of pre-scriptions and habits common to all the writers of a period. Which means that a language is a kind of natural ambience wholly pervading the writer's expression, yet without endowing it with form or content: it is, as it were, an abstract circle of truths, outside of which alone the solid residue of an individual *logos* begins to settle. It enfolds the whole of literary creation much as the earth, the sky and the line where they meet outline a familiar habitat for mankind. It is not so much a stock of materials as a horizon, which implies both a boundary and a perspective; in short, it is the comforting area of an ordered space. The writer literally takes nothing from it; a language is for him rather a frontier, to overstep which alone might lead to the linguistically super-natural; it is a field of action, the definition of, and hope for, a possibility. It is not the locus of a social commitment, but merely a reflex response involving no choice, the undivided property of men, not of writers; it remains outside the ritual of Letters; it is a social object by definition, not by option. No one can without formalities pretend to insert his freedom as a writer into the resistant medium of language because, behind the latter, the whole of History stands unified and complete in the manner of a Natural Order. Hence, for the writer, a language is nothing but a human horizon which provides a distant setting of *familiarity*, the value of which, incidentally, is entirely negative: to say that Camus and Queneau speak the same language is merely to presume, by a differential operation, all languages, archaic and futuristic, that they do not use. Suspended between forms either disused or as yet unknown, the writer's language is not so much a fund to be drawn on as an extreme limit; it is the geometrical *locus* of all that he could not say without, like Orpheus looking back, losing the stable meaning of his enterprise and his essential gesture as a social being.

A language is therefore on the hither side of Literature. Style is almost beyond it: imagery, delivery, vocabulary spring from the body and the past of the writer and gradually become the very reflexes of his art. Thus under the name of style a self-sufficient language is evolved which has its roots only in the depths of the author's personal and secret mythology, that subnature of expression where the first coition of words and things takes place, where once and for all the great verbal themes of his existence come to be installed. Whatever its sophistication, style has always something crude about it: it is a form with no clear destination, the product of a thrust, not an intention, and, as it were, a vertical and lonely dimension of thought. Its frame of reference is biological or biographical, not historical: it is the writer's 'thing', his glory and his prison, it is his solitude. Indifferent to society and transparent to it, a closed personal process, it is in no way the product of a choice or of a reflection on Literature. It is the private portion of the ritual, it rises up from the writer's myth-laden depths and unfolds beyond his area of control. It is the decorative voice of hidden, secret flesh; it works as does Necessity, as if, in this kind of floral growth, style were no more than the outcome of a blind and stubborn metamorphosis starting from a sub-language elaborated where flesh and external reality come together. Style is properly speaking a germinative phenomenon, the transmutation of a Humour. Hence stylistic overtones are distributed in depth; whereas speech has a horizontal structure, its secrets are on a level with the words in which they are couched, and what it conceals is revealed by the very duration of its flow. In speech, everything is held forth, meant for immediate consumption, and words, silences and their common mobility are launched towards a meaning superseded: it is a transfer leaving no trace and brooking no delay. Style, on the other hand, has only a vertical dimension, it plunges into the closed recollection of the person and achieves its opacity from a certain experience of matter; style is never anything but metaphor, that is, equivalence of the author's literary intention and carnal structure (it must be remembered that structure is the residual deposit of duration). So that style is always a secret; but the occult aspect of its implications does not arise from the mobile and ever-provisional nature of language; its secret is recollection locked within the body of the writer. The allusive virtue of style is not a matter of speed, as in speech, where what is unsaid nevertheless remains as an interim of language, but a matter of density, for what stands firmly and deeply beneath style, brought together harshly or tenderly in its figures of speech, are fragments of a reality entirely alien to language. The miracle of this transmutation makes style a kind of supra-literary operation which carries man to the threshold of power and magic. By reason of its biological origin, style resides outside art, that is, outside the pact which binds the writer to society. Authors may therefore be imagined who prefer the security of art to the loneliness of style. The very type of an author without a style is Gide, whose craftsmanlike approach exploits the pleasure the moderns derive from a certain classical ethos, just as Saint-Saëns has composed in Bach's idiom, or Poulenc in Schubert's. In contrast, modern poetry – such as Hugo's, Rimbaud's or Char's – is saturated with style and is *art* only by virtue of an intention to be Poetry. It is the Authority of style, that is, the entirely free relationship between language and its fleshly double, which places the writer above History as the freshness of Innocence.

A language is therefore a horizon, and style a vertical dimension, which together map out for the writer a Nature, since he does not choose either. The language functions negatively, as the initial limit of the possible, style is a Necessity which binds the writer's humour to his form of expression. In the former, he finds a familiar History, in the latter, a familiar personal past. In both cases he deals with a Nature, that is, a familiar repertory of gestures, a gestuary, as it were, in which the energy expended is purely operative, serving here to enumerate, there to transform, but never to appraise or signify a choice. Now every Form is also a Value, which is why there is room, between a language and a style, for another formal reality: writing. Within any literary form, there is a general choice of tone, of ethos, if you like, and this is precisely where the writer shows himself clearly as an individual because this is where he commits himself. A language and a style are data prior to all problematics of language, they are the natural product of Time and of the person as a biological entity; but the formal identity of the writer is truly established only outside the permanence of grammatical norms and stylistic constants, where the written continuum, first collected and enclosed within a perfectly innocent linguistic nature, at last becomes a total sign, the choice of a human attitude, the affirmation of a certain Good. It thus commits the writer to manifest and communicate a state of happiness or malaise, and links the form of his utterance, which is at once normal and singular, to the vast History of the Others. A language and a style are blind forces; a mode of writing is an act of historical solidarity. A language and a style are objects; a mode of writing is a function: it is the relationship between creation and society, the literary language transformed by its social finality, form considered as a human intention and thus linked to the great crises of History. Mérimée and Fénelon, for instance, are separated by linguistic phenomena and contingent features of style; yet they make use of a language charged with the same intentionality, their ideas of form and content share a common framework, they accept the same type of conventions, the same technical reflexes work through both of them. Although separated by a century and a half, they use exactly the same instrument in the same way: an instrument perhaps a little changed in outward appearance, but not at all in the place and manner of its employment. In short, they have the same mode of writing. In contrast, writers who are almost contemporaries, Mérimée and Lautréamont, Mallarmé and Céline, Gide and Queneau, Claudel and Camus, who have shared or who share our language at the same stage of its historical development use utterly different modes of writing. Everything separates them: tone, delivery, purpose, ethos, and naturalness of expression: the conclusion is that to live at the same time and share the same language is a small matter compared with modes of writing so dissimilar and so sharply defined by their very dissimilarity.

These modes of writing, though different, are comparable, because they owe their existence to one identical process, namely the writer's consideration of the social use which he has chosen for his form, and his commitment to this choice. Placed at the centre of the problematics of literature, which cannot exist prior to it, writing is thus essentially the morality of form, the choice of that social area within which the writer elects to situate the Nature of his language. But this social area is by no means that of an actual consumption. It is not a question for the writer of choosing the social group for which he is to write: well he knows that, save for the possibility of a Revolution, it can only be for the self same society. His choice is a matter of conscience, not of efficacy. His writing is a way of conceiving Literature, not of extending its limits. Or better still: it is because the writer cannot modify in any way the objective data which govern the consumption of literature (these purely historical data are beyond his control even if he is aware of them), that he voluntarily places the need for a free language at the sources of this language and not in its eventual consumption. So that writing is an ambiguous reality : on the one hand, it unquestionably arises from a confrontation of the writer with the society of his time; on the other hand, from this social finality, it refers the writer back, by a sort of tragic reversal, to the sources, that is to say, the instruments of creation. Failing the power to supply him with a freely consumed language, History suggests to him the demand for one freely produced.

Thus the choice of, and afterwards the responsibility for, a mode of writing point to the presence of Freedom, but this Freedom has not the same limits at different moments of History. It is not granted to the writer to choose his mode of writing from a kind of non-temporal store of literary forms. It is under the pressure of History and Tradition that the possible modes of writing for a given writer are established; there is a History of Writing. But this History is dual : at the very moment when general History proposes – or imposes – new problematics of the literary language, writing still remains full of the recollection of previous usage, for language is never innocent : words have a second-order memory which mysteriously persists in the midst of new meanings. Writing is precisely this compromise between freedom and remembrance, it is this freedom which remembers and is free only in the gesture of choice, but is no longer so within duration. True, I can today select such and such mode of writing, and in so doing assert my freedom, aspire to the freshness of novelty or to a tradition; but it is impossible to develop it within duration without gradually becoming a prisoner of someone else's words and even of my own. A stubborn after-image, which comes from all the previous modes of writing and even from the past of my own, drowns the sound of my present words. Any written trace precipitates, as inside a chemical at first transparent, innocent and neutral, mere duration gradually reveals in suspension a whole past of increasing density, like a cryptogram.

Writing as Freedom is therefore a mere moment. But this moment is one of the most explicit in History, since History is always and above all a choice and the limits of this choice. It is because writing derives from a meaningful gesture of the writer that it reaches the deeper layers of History, much more palpably than does any other cross-section of literature. The unity of classical writing, which remained uniform for centuries, the plurality of its modes in modern times, increased in the last hundred years until it came near to questioning the very fact of literature, this kind of disintegration of French writing does indeed correspond to a great crisis in general History, which is noticeable in literary History proper, only much more confusedly. What separates the 'thought' of a Balzac from that of a Flaubert is a variation within the same school; what contrasts their modes of writing is an essential break, at the precise moment when a new economic structure is joined on to an older one, thereby bringing about decisive changes in mentality and consciousness.

POLITICAL MODES OF
WRITING

All modes of writing have in common the fact of being 'closed' and thus different from spoken language. Writing is in no way an instrument for communication, it is not an open route through which there passes only the intention to speak. A whole disorder flows through speech and gives it this self-devouring momentum which keeps it in a perpetually suspended state. Conversely, writing is a hardened language which is self-contained and is in no way meant to deliver to its own duration a mobile series of approximations. It is on the contrary meant to impose, thanks to the shadow cast by its system of signs, the image of a speech which had a structure even before it came into existence. What makes writing the opposite of speech is that the former always *appears* symbolical, introverted, ostensibly turned towards an occult side of language, whereas the second is nothing but a flow of empty signs, the movement of which alone is significant. The whole of speech is epitomized in this expendability of words, in this froth ceaselessly swept onwards, and speech is found only where language self-evidently functions like a devouring process which swallows only the moving crest of the words. Writing, on the contrary, is always rooted in something beyond language, it develops like a seed, not like a line, it manifests an essence and holds the threat of a secret, it is an anti-communication, it is intimidating. All writing will therefore contain the ambiguity of an object which is both language and coercion: there exists fundamentally in writing a 'circumstance' foreign to language, there is, as it were, the weight of a gaze conveying an intention which is no longer linguistic. This gaze may well express a passion of language, as in literary modes of writing; it may also express the threat of retribution, as in political ones: writing is then meant to unite at a single stroke the reality of the acts and the ideality of the ends. This is why power, or the shadow cast by power, always ends in creating an axiological writing, in which the distance which usually separates fact from value disappears within the very space of the word, which is given at once as description and as judgment. The word becomes an alibi, that is, an elsewhere and a justification. This, which is true of the literary modes of writing, in which the unity of the signs is ceaselessly fascinated by zones of infra- or ultra-language, is even truer of the political ones, in which the alibi stemming from language is at the same time intimidation and glorification: for it is power or conflict which produce the purest types of writing.

We shall see later that classical writing was a ceremonial which manifested the implantation of the writer into a particular political society, and that to speak like Vaugelas meant in the first place to be connected with the exercise of power. The Revolution did not modify the norms of this writing, since its force of thinkers remained, all things considered, the same, having merely passed from intellectual to political power; but the exceptional conditions of the struggle nevertheless brought about, within the great Form of classicism, a revolutionary mode of writing proper, defined not by its structure (which was more conventional than ever) but by its closed character and by its counterpart, since the use of language was then linked, as never before in history, to the Blood which had been shed. The Revolutionaries had no reason to wish to alter classical writing; they were in no way aware of questioning the nature of man, still less his language, and an 'instrument' they had inherited from Voltaire, Rousseau or Vauvenargues could not appear to them as compromised. It was the singularity of the historical circumstances which produced the identity of the revolutionary mode of writing. Baudelaire spoke somewhere of the 'grandiloquent truth of gestures on life's great occasions'. The Revolution was in the highest degree one of those great occasions when truth, through the bloodshed that it costs, becomes so weighty that its expression demands the very forms of theatrical amplification.

Revolutionary writing was the one and only grand
gesture commensurate with the daily presence of the
guillotine. What today appears turgid was then no
more than life-size. This writing, which bears all the
signs of inflation, was an exact writing: never was
language more incredible, yet never was it less spurious. This grandiloquence was not only form modelled
on drama; it was also the awareness of it. Without
this extravagant pose, typical of all the great revolutionaries, which enabled Guadet, the Girondin, when
arrested at Saint-Emilion, to declare without looking
ridiculous, since he was about to die: 'Yes, I am
Guadet. Executioner, do your duty. Go take my head
to the tyrants of my country. It has always turned
them pale; once severed, it will turn them paler still',
the Revolution could not have been this mythical
event which made History fruitful, along with all
future ideas on revolution. Revolutionary writing was
so to speak the entelechy of the revolutionary
legend: it struck fear into men's hearts and imposed
upon them a citizen's sacrament of Bloodshed.

Marxist writing is of a different order. Here the
closed character of the form does not derive from
rhetorical amplification or from grandiloquence in
delivery, but from a lexicon as specialized and as
functional as a technical vocabulary; even metaphors

are here severely codified. French revolutionary writing always proclaimed a right founded on bloodshed or moral justification, whereas from the very start Marxist writing is presented as the language of knowledge. Here, writing is univocal, because it is meant to maintain the cohesion of a Nature; it is the lexical identity of this writing which allows it to impose a stability in its explanations and a permanence in its method; it is only in the light of its whole linguistic system that Marxism is perceived in all its political implications. Marxist writing is as much given to understatement as revolutionary writing is to grandiloquence, since each word is no longer anything but a narrow reference to the set of principles which tacitly underlie it. For instance, the word 'imply', frequently encountered in Marxist writing, does not there have its neutral dictionary meaning; it always refers to a precise historical process, and is like an algebraical sign representing a whole bracketed set of previous postulates.

Being linked to action, Marxist writing has rapidly become, in fact, a language expressing value-judgments. This character, already visible in Marx, whose writing however remains in general explanatory, has come to pervade writing completely in the era of triumphant Stalinism. Certain outwardly similar notions, for which a neutral vocabulary would not seek a dual designation, are evaluatively parted from each other, so that each element gravitates towards a different noun : for instance, 'cosmopolitanism' is the negative of 'internationalism' (already in Marx). In the Stalinist world, in which *definition*, that is to say the separation between Good and Evil, becomes the sole content of all language, there are no more words without values attached to them, so that finally the function of writing is to cut out one stage of a process : there is no more lapse of time between naming and judging, and the closed character of language is perfected, since in the last analysis it is a value which is given as explanation of another value. For instance, it may be alleged that such and such a criminal has engaged in activities harmful to the interests of the state; which boils down to saying that a criminal is someone who commits a crime. We see that this is in fact a tautology, a device constantly used in Stalinist writing. For the latter no longer aims at founding a Marxist version of the facts, or a revolutionary rationale of actions, but at presenting reality in a pre-judged form, thus imposing a reading which involves immediate condemnation : the objective content of the word 'deviationist' puts it into a penological category. If two deviationists band together, they become 'fractionists', which does not involve an objectively different crime, but an increase in the sentence imposed. One can enumerate a properly Marxist writing (that of Marx and Lenin) and a writing of triumphant Stalinism; there certainly is as well a Trotskyist writing and a tactical writing, for instance that of the French Communist party with its substitution of 'people', then of 'plain folk', for 'working class', and the wilful ambiguity of terms like 'democracy', 'freedom', 'peace', etc.

There is no doubt at all that each regime has its own writing, no history of which has yet been written. Since writing is the spectacular commitment of language, it contains at one and the same time, thanks to a valuable ambiguity, the reality and the appearance of power, what it is, and what it would like to be thought to be : a history of political modes of writing would therefore be the best of social phenomenologies. For instance, the French Restoration evolved a class writing by means of which repression was immediately given as a condemnation spontaneously arising from classical 'Nature' : workers claiming rights were always 'troublemakers', strike-breakers were 'good workmen', and the subservience of judges became, in this language, the 'paternal vigilance of magistrates' (it is thanks to a similar procedure that Gaullism today calls Communists 'separatists'). We see that here the function of writing is to maintain a clear conscience and that its mission is fraudulently to identify the original fact with its remotest subsequent transformation by bolstering up the justification of actions with the additional guarantee of its own reality. This fact about writing is, by the way, typical of all authoritarian regimes; it is what might be called police-state writing: we know, for example, that the content of the word 'Order' always indicates repression.

The spreading influence of political and social facts into the literary field of consciousness has produced a new type of scriptor, halfway between the party member and the writer, deriving from the former an ideal image of committed man, and from the latter the notion that a written work is an act. Thus while the intellectual supersedes the writer, there appears in periodicals and in essays a militant mode of writing entirely freed from stylistic considerations, and which is, so to speak, a professional language signifying 'presence'. In this mode of writing, nuances abound. Nobody will deny that there is such a thing, for instance, as a writing typical of *Esprit* or of *Les Temps Modernes*.* What these intellectual modes of writing have in common, is that in them language, instead of being a privileged area, tends to become the sufficient sign of commitment. To come to adopt a closed sphere of language under the pressure of all those who do not speak it, is to proclaim one's act of choosing, if not necessarily one's agreement with that choice. Writing here resembles the signature one

* *Esprit* and *Les Temps Modernes* are two prominent monthlies, the first Left-wing Catholic and the second directed by J.-P. Sartre.

affixes at the foot of a collective proclamation one has not written oneself. So that to adopt a mode of writing – or, even better, to make it one's own – means to save oneself all the preliminaries of a choice, and to make it quite clear that one takes for granted the reasons for such a choice. Any intellectual writing is therefore the first of the 'leaps of the intellect'. Whereas an ideally free language never could function as a sign of my own person and would give no information whatsoever about my history and my freedom, the writing to which I entrust myself already exists entirely as an institution; it reveals my past and my choice, it gives me a history, it blazons forth my situation, it commits me without my having to declare the fact. Form thus becomes more than ever an autonomous object, meant to signify a property which is collective and protected, and this object is a trouble-saving device: it functions as an economy signal whereby the scriptor constantly imposes his conversion without ever revealing how it came about.

This duplicity of today's intellectual modes of writing is emphasized by the fact that in spite of the efforts made in our time, it has proved impossible successfully to liquidate Literature entirely: it still constitutes a verbal horizon commanding respect. The intellectual is still only an incompletely transformed writer, and unless he scuttles himself and becomes for ever a militant who no longer writes (some have done so, and are therefore forgotten), he cannot but come back to the fascination of former modes of writing, transmitted through Literature as an instrument intact but obsolete. These intellectual modes of writing are therefore unstable, they remain literary to the extent that they are powerless, and are political only through their obsession with commitment. In short, we are still dealing with ethical modes of writing, in which the conscience of the scriptor (one no longer ventures to call him a writer) finds the comforting image of collective salvation.

But just as, in the present state of History, any political mode of writing can only uphold a police world, so any intellectual mode of writing can only give rise to a para-literature, which no longer dares to speak its name. Both are therefore in a complete blind alley, they can lead only to complicity or impotence, which means, in either case, to alienation.

WRITING AND THE NOVEL

The Novel and History have been closely related in the very century which witnessed their greatest development. Their link in depth, that which should allow us to understand at once Balzac and Michelet, is that in both we find the construction of an autarkic world which elaborates its own dimensions and limits, and organizes within these its own Time, its own Space, its population, its own set of objects and its myths.

This sphericity of the great works of the nineteenth century found its expression in those long recitatives, the Novel and History, which are, as it were, plane projections of a curved and organic world of which the serial story which came into being at that precise moment, presents, through its involved complications, a degraded image. And yet narration is not necessarily a law of the form. A whole period could conceive novels in letters, for instance; and another can evolve a practice of History by means of analyses. Therefore Narration, as a form common to both the Novel and to History, does remain, in general, the choice or the expression of an historical moment.

Obsolete in spoken French, the preterite, which is the cornerstone of Narration, always signifies the presence of Art; it is a part of a ritual of Letters. Its function is no longer that of a tense. The part it plays is to reduce reality to a point of time, and to abstract, from the depth of a multiplicity of experiences, a pure verbal act, freed from the existential roots of knowledge, and directed towards a logical link with other acts, other processes, a general movement of the world: it aims at maintaining a hierarchy in the realm of facts. Through the preterite, the verb implicitly belongs with a causal chain, it partakes of a set of related and orientated actions, it functions as the algebraic sign of an intention. Allowing as it does an ambiguity between temporality and causality, it calls for a sequence of events, that is, for an intelligible Narrative. This is why it is the ideal instrument for every construction of a world; it is the unreal time of cosmogonies, myths, History and Novels. It presupposes a world which is constructed, elaborated, self-sufficient, reduced to significant lines, and not one which has been sent sprawling before us, for us to take or leave. Behind the preterite there always lurks a demiurge, a God or a reciter. The world is not unexplained since it is told like a story; each one of its accidents is but a circumstance, and the preterite is precisely this operative sign whereby the narrator reduces the exploded reality to a slim and pure logos, without density, without volume, without spread, and whose sole function is to unite as rapidly as possible a cause and an end. When the historian states that the duc de Guise died on December 23rd, 1588, or when the novelist relates that the Marchioness went out at five o'clock,* such actions emerge from a past without substance; purged of the uncertainty of existence, they have the stability and outline of an algebra, they are a recollection, but a useful recollection, the interest of which far surpasses its duration.

So that finally the preterite is the expression of an order, and consequently of a euphoria. Thanks to it, reality is neither mysterious nor absurd; it is clear, almost familiar, repeatedly gathered up and contained in the hand of a creator; it is subjected to the ingenious pressure of his freedom. For all the great storytellers of the nineteenth century, the world may be full of pathos but it is not derelict, since it is a grouping of coherent relations, since there is no overlapping between the written facts, since he who tells the story has the power to do away with the opacity and the solitude of the existences which made it up, since he can in all sentences bear witness to a communication and a hierarchy of actions and since, to tell the truth, these very actions can be reduced to mere signs.

* The sentence which for Valéry epitomized the conventions of the novel.

The narrative past is therefore a part of a security system for Belles-Lettres. Being the image of an order, it is one of those numerous formal pacts made between the writer and society for the justification of the former and the serenity of the latter. The preterite *signifies* a creation: that is, it proclaims and imposes it. Even from the depth of the most sombre realism, it has a reassuring effect because, thanks to it, the verb expresses a closed, well-defined, substantival act, the Novel has a name, it escapes the terror of an expression without laws: reality becomes slighter and more familiar, it fits within a style, it does not outrun language. Literature remains the currency in use in a society apprised, by the very form of words, of the meaning of what it consumes. On the contrary, when the Narrative is rejected in favour of other literary genres, or when, within the narration, the preterite is replaced by less ornamental forms, fresher, more full-blooded and nearer to speech (the present tense or the present perfect), Literature becomes the receptacle of existence in all its density and no longer of its meaning alone. The acts it recounts are still separated from History, but no longer from people.

We now understand what is profitable and what is intolerable in the preterite as used in the Novel: it is a lie made manifest, it delineates an area of plausibility which reveals the possible in the very act of unmasking it as false. The teleology common to the

Novel and to narrated History is the alienation of the facts: the preterite is the very act by which society affirms its possession of its past and its possibility. It creates a content credible, yet flaunted as an illusion; it is the ultimate term of a formal dialectics which clothes an unreal fact in the garb first of truth then of a lie denounced as such. This has to be related to a certain mythology of the universal typifying the bourgeois society of which the Novel is a character- istic product; it involves giving to the imaginary the formal guarantee of the real, but while preserving in the sign the ambiguity of a double object, at once believable and false. This operation occurs constantly in the whole of Western art, in which the false is equal to the true, not through any agnosticism or poetic duplicity, but because the true is supposed to contain a germ of the universal, or to put it differ- ently, an essence capable of fecundating by mere re- production, several orders of things among which some differ by their remoteness and some by their fictitious character.

It is thanks to an expedient of the same kind that the triumphant bourgeoisie of the last century was able to look upon its values as universal and to carry over to sections of society which were absolutely heterogeneous to it all the Names which were parts of its ethos. This is strictly how myths function, and the Novel – and within the Novel, the preterite – are mythological objects in which there is, superimposed

33

upon an immediate intention, a second-order appeal to a corpus of dogmas, or better, to a pedagogy, since what is sought is to impart an essence in the guise of an artefact. In order to grasp the significance of the preterite, we have but to compare the Western art of the novel with a certain Chinese tradition, for instance, in which art lies solely in the perfection with which reality is imitated. But in this tradition no sign, absolutely nothing, must allow any distinction to be drawn between the natural and the artificial objects : this wooden walnut must not impart to me, along with the image of a walnut, the intention of conveying to me the art which gave birth to it. Whereas on the contrary this is what writing does in the novel. Its task is to put the mask in place and at the same time to point it out.

This ambiguous function disclosed in the preterite is found in another fact relating to this type of writing : the third person in the Novel. The reader will perhaps recall a novel by Agatha Christie in which all the invention consisted in concealing the murderer beneath the use of the first person of the narrative. The reader looked for him behind every 'he' in the plot : he was all the time hidden under the 'I'. Agatha Christie knew perfectly well that, in the novel, the 'I' is usually a spectator, and that it is the 'he' who is the actor. Why? The 'he' is a typical novelistic convention; like the narrative tense, it signifies and carries through the action of the novel; if the third person is absent, the novel is powerless to come into being, and even wills its own destruction. The 'he' is a formal manifestation of the myth, and we have just seen that, in the West at least, there is no art which does not point to its own mask. The third person, like the preterite, therefore performs this service for the art of the novel, and supplies its consumers with the security born of a credible fabrication which is yet constantly held up as false.

Less ambiguous, the 'I' is thereby less typical of the novel: it is therefore at the same time the most obvious solution, when the narration remains on this side of convention (Proust's work, for instance, purports to be a mere introduction to Literature), and the most sophisticated, when the 'I' takes its place beyond convention and attempts to destroy it, by conferring on the narrative the spurious naturalness of taking the reader into its confidence (such is the guileful air of some stories by Gide). In the same way the use of the 'he' in a novel involves two opposed systems of ethics: since it represents an unquestioned convention, it attracts the most conformist and the least dissatisfied, as well as those others who have decided that, finally, this convention is necessary to the novelty of their work. In any case, it is the sign of an intelligible pact between society and the author;

but it is also, for the latter, the most important means he has of building the world in the way that he chooses. It is therefore more than a literary experiment: it is a human act which connects creation to History or to existence.

In Balzac for instance, the multiplicity of 'he's', this vast network of characters, slight in terms of solid flesh, but consistent by the duration of their acts, reveals the existence of a world of which History is the first datum. The Balzacian 'he' is not the end-product of a development starting from some transformed and generalized 'I'; it is the original and crude element of the novel, the material, not the outcome, the creative activity: there is no Balzacian history prior to the history of each third person in the novels of Balzac. His 'he' is analogous to Caesar's 'he': the third person here brings about a kind of algebraic state of the action, in which existence plays the smallest possible part, in favour of elements which connect, clarify, or show the tragedy inherent in human relationships. Conversely – or at any rate previously – the function of 'he' in the novel can be that of expressing an existential experience. In many modern novelists the history of the man is identified with the course of the conjugation: starting from an 'I' which is still the form which expresses anonymity most faithfully, man and author little by little win the right to the third person, in proportion as existence becomes fate, and soliloquy becomes a

Novel. Here the appearance of the 'he' is not the starting point of History, it is the end of an effort which has been successful in extracting from a personal world made up of humours and tendencies, a form which is pure, significant, and which therefore vanishes as soon as it is born thanks to the totally conventional and ethereal decor of the third person. This certainly was the course displayed in the first novels of Jean Cayrol whose case can be taken as an exemplar. But whereas in the classics – and we know that where writing is concerned classicism lasts until Flaubert – the withdrawal of the biological person testifies to the establishment of essential man, in novelists such as Cayrol, the invasion of the 'he' is a progressive conquest over the profound darkness of the existential 'I': so true it is that the Novel, identified as it is by its most formal signs, is a gesture of sociability; it establishes Literature as an institution.

Maurice Blanchot has shown, in the case of Kafka, that the elaboration of the impersonal narrative (let us notice, apropos of this term, that the 'third person' is always presented as a negative degree of the person) was an act of fidelity to the essence of language, since the latter naturally tends towards its own destruction. We therefore understand how 'he' is a victory over 'I', inasmuch as it conjures up a state at once more literary and more absent. None the less this victory is ceaselessly threatened: the literary convention of the 'he' is necessary to the belittling of the person, but runs at every moment the risk of encumbering it with an unexpected density. For Literature is like phosphorus: it shines with its maximum brilliance at the moment when it attempts to die. But as, on the other hand, it is an act which necessarily implies a duration – especially in the Novel – there can never be any Novel independently of Belles-Lettres. So that the third person in the Novel is one of the most obsessive signs of this tragic aspect of writing which was born in the last century, when under the weight of History, Literature became dissociated from the society which consumes it. Between the third person as used by Balzac and that used by Flaubert, there is a world of difference (that of 1848): in the former we have a view of History which is harsh, but coherent and certain of its principles, the triumph of an order; in the latter, an art which in order to escape its pangs of conscience either exaggerates conventions or frantically attempts to destroy them. Modernism begins with the search for a Literature which is no longer possible.

Thus we find, in the Novel too, this machinery directed towards both destruction and resurrection, and typical of the whole of modern art. What must be destroyed is duration, that is, the ineffable binding force running through existence: for order, whether

it be that of poetic flow or of narrative signs, that of
Terror or plausibility, is always a murder in intention. But what reconquers the writer is again duration, for it is impossible to develop a negative within
time, without elaborating a positive art, an order
which must be destroyed anew. So that the greater
modern works linger as long as possible, in a sort of
miraculous stasis, on the threshold of Literature, in
this anticipatory state in which the breadth of life is
given, stretched but not yet destroyed by this crowning phase, an order of signs. For instance, we have the
first person in Proust, whose whole work rests on a
slow and protracted effort towards Literature. We
have Jean Cayrol, whose acquiescence to the Novel
comes only as the very last stage of soliloquy, as if
the literary act, being supremely ambiguous, could be
delivered of a creation consecrated by society, only at
the moment when it has at last succeeded in destroying the existential density of a hitherto meaningless
duration.

The Novel is a Death; it transforms life into
destiny, a memory into a useful act, duration into an
orientated and meaningful time. But this transformation can be accomplished only in full view of society.
It is society which imposes the Novel, that is, a complex of signs, as a transcendence and as the History of
a duration. It is therefore by the obviousness of its
intention, grasped in that of the narrative signs, that
one can recognize the path which, through all the

solemnity of art, binds the writer to society. The preterite and the third person in the Novel are nothing but the fateful gesture with which the writer draws attention to the mask which he is wearing. The whole of Literature can declare *Larvatus prodeo*,* As I walk forward, I point out my mask. Whether we deal with the inhuman experience of the poet, who accepts the most momentous of all breaks, that from the language of society, or with the plausible untruth of the novelist, sincerity here feels a need of the signs of falsehood, and of conspicuous falsehood in order to last and to be consumed. Writing is the product, and ultimately the source, of this ambiguity. This specialized language, the use of which gives the writer a glorious but none the less superintended function, evinces a kind of servitude, invisible at first, which characterizes any responsibility. Writing, free in its beginnings, is finally the bond which links the writer to a History which is itself in chains: society stamps upon him the unmistakable signs of art so as to draw him along the more inescapably in its own process of alienation.

---

* *Larvatus prodeo* was the motto of Descartes.

IS THERE ANY POETIC
WRITING?

In the classical period, prose and poetry are quantities, their difference can be measured; they are neither more nor less separated than two different numbers, contiguous like them, but dissimilar because of the very difference in their magnitudes. If I use the word prose for a minimal form of speech, the most economical vehicle for thought, and if I use the letters a, b, c for certain attributes of language, which are useless but decorative, such as metre, rhyme or the ritual of images, all the linguistic surface will be accounted for in M. Jourdain's* double equation:

$$Poetry = Prose + a + b + c$$
$$Prose = Poetry - a - b - c$$

whence it clearly follows that Poetry is always different from Prose. But this difference is not one of essence, it is one of quantity. It does not, therefore, jeopardize the unity of language, which is an article of classical dogma. One may effect a different dosage in manner of speech, according to the social occasion: here, prose or rhetoric, there, poetry or precosity, in

* Molière's *Bourgeois Gentilhomme*.

accordance with a whole ritual of expression laid down by good society, but there remains everywhere a single language, which reflects the eternal categories of the mind. Classical poetry is felt to be merely an ornamental variation of prose, the fruit of an *art* (that is, a technique), never a different language, or the product of a particular sensibility. Any poetry is then only the decorative equation, whether allusive or forced, of a possible prose which is latent, virtually and potentially, in any conceivable manner of expression. 'Poetic', in the days of classicism, never evokes any particular domain, any particular depth of feeling, any special coherence, or separate universe, but only an individual handling of a verbal technique, that of 'expressing oneself' according to rules more artistic, therefore more sociable, than those of conversation, in other terms, the technique of projecting out an inner thought, springing fully armed from the Mind, a speech which is made more socially acceptable by virtue of the very conspicuousness of its conventions.

We know that nothing of this structure remains in modern poetry, which springs not from Baudelaire but from Rimbaud, unless it is in cases where one takes up again, in a revised traditional mode, the formal imperatives of classical poetry: henceforth, poets give to their speech the status of a closed Nature, which covers both the function and the structure of language. Poetry is then no longer a Prose either ornamental or shorn of liberties. It is a quality *sui generis* and without antecedents. It is no longer an attribute but a substance, and therefore it can very well renounce signs, since it carries its own nature within itself, and does not need to signal its identity outwardly: poetic language and prosaic language are sufficiently separate to be able to dispense with the very signs of their difference.

Furthermore, the alleged relations between thought and language are reversed; in classical art, a ready-made thought generates an utterance which 'expresses' or 'translates' it. Classical thought is devoid of duration, classical poetry has it only in such degree as is necessary to its technical arrangement. In modern poetics, on the contrary, words produce a kind of formal continuum from which there gradually emanates an intellectual or emotional density which would have been impossible without them; speech is then the solidified time of a more spiritual gestation, during which the 'thought' is prepared, installed little by little by the contingency of words. This verbal luck, which will bring down the ripe fruit of a meaning, presupposes therefore a poetic time which is no longer that of a 'fabrication', but that of a possible adventure, the meeting-point of a sign and an intention. Modern poetry is opposed to classical art by a difference which involves the whole structure of language, without leaving between those two types of poetry anything in common except the same sociological intention.

The economy of classical language (Prose and Poetry) is relational, which means that in it words are abstracted as much as possible in the interest of relationships. In it, no word has a density by itself, it is hardly the sign of a thing, but rather the means of conveying a connection. Far from plunging into an inner reality consubstantial to its outer configuration, it extends, as soon as it is uttered, towards other words, so as to form a superficial chain of intentions. A glance at the language of mathematics will perhaps enable us to grasp the relational nature of classical prose and poetry: we know that in mathematical language, not only is each quantity provided with a sign, but also that the relations between these quantities are themselves transcribed, by means of a sign expressing operative equality or difference. It may be said that the whole movement of mathematical flow derives from an explicit reading of its relations. The language of classicism is animated by an analogous, although of course less rigid, movement: its 'words', neutralized, made absent by rigorous recourse to a tradition which dessicates their freshness, avoid the phonetic or semantic accident which would concentrate the flavour of language at one point and halt its

intellectual momentum in the interest of an un-
equally distributed enjoyment. The classical flow is a
succession of elements whose density is even; it is ex-
posed to the same emotional pressure, and relieves
those elements of any tendency towards an individual
meaning appearing at all invented. The poetic vocabulary itself is one of usage, not of invention : images in
it are recognizable in a body; they do not exist in
isolation; they are due to long custom, not to individual creation. The function of the classical poet
is not therefore to find new words, with more body
or more brilliance, but to follow the order of an
ancient ritual, to perfect the symmetry or the conciseness of a relation, to bring a thought exactly
within the compass of a metre. Classical conceits involve relations, not words : they belong to an art of
expression, not of invention. The words, here, do not,
as they later do, thanks to a kind of violent and unexpected abruptness, reproduce the depth and singularity of an individual experience; they are spread out
to form a surface, according to the exigencies of an
elegant or decorative purpose. They delight us because of the formulation which brings them together,
not because of their own power or beauty.

True, classical language does not reach the functional perfection of the relational network of mathematics : relations are not signified, in it, by any
special signs, but only by accidents of form and disposition. It is the restraint of the words in itself, their

alignment, which achieves the relational nature of classical discourse. Overworked in a restricted number of ever-similar relations, classical words are on the way to becoming an algebra where rhetorical figures of speech, clichés, function as virtual linking devices; they have lost their density and gained a more interrelated state of speech; they operate in the manner of chemical valences, outlining a verbal area full of symmetrical connections, junctions and networks from which arise, without the respite afforded by wonder, fresh intentions towards signification. Hardly have the fragments of classical discourse yielded their meaning than they become messengers or harbingers, carrying ever further a meaning which refuses to settle within the depths of a word, but tries instead to spread widely enough to become a total gesture of intellection, that is, of communication.

Now the distortion to which Hugo tried to subject the alexandrine, which is of all meters the most interrelational, already contains the whole future of modern poetry, since what is attempted is to eliminate the intention to establish relationships and to produce instead an explosion of words. For modern poetry, since it must be distinguished from classical poetry and from any type of prose, destroys the spontaneously functional nature of language, and leaves standing only its lexical basis. It retains only the outward shape of relationships, their music, but not their reality. The Word shines forth above a line of relationships emptied of their content, grammar is bereft of its purpose, it becomes prosody and is no longer anything but an inflexion which lasts only to present the Word. Connections are not properly speaking abolished, they are merely reserved areas, a parody of themselves, and this void is necessary for the density of the Word to rise out of a magic vacuum, like a sound and a sign devoid of background, like 'fury and mystery'.

In classical speech, connections lead the word on, and at once carry it towards a meaning which is an ever-deferred project; in modern poetry, connections are only an extension of the word, it is the Word which is 'the dwelling place', it is rooted like a *fons et origo* in the prosody of functions, which are perceived but unreal. Here, connections only fascinate, and it is the Word which gratifies and fulfills like the sudden revelation of a truth. To say that this truth is of a poetic order is merely to say that the Word in poetry can never be untrue, because it is a whole; it shines with an infinite freedom and prepares to radiate towards innumerable uncertain and possible connections. Fixed connections being abolished, the word is left only with a vertical project, it is like a monolith, or a pillar which plunges into a totality of meanings, reflexes and recollections: it is a sign which stands. The poetic word is here an act without immediate past, without environment, and which holds forth only the dense shadow of reflexes from all sources which are associated with it. Thus under each Word in modern poetry there lies a sort of existential geology, in which is gathered the total content of the Name, instead of a chosen content as in classical prose and poetry. The Word is no longer guided *in advance* by the general intention of a socialized discourse; the consumer of poetry, deprived of the guide of selective connections, encounters the Word frontally, and receives it as an absolute quantity, accompanied by all its possible associations. The Word, here, is encyclopaedic, it contains simultaneously all the acceptations from which a relational discourse might have required it to choose. It therefore achieves a state which is possible only in the dictionary or in poetry – places where the noun can live without its article – and is reduced to a sort of zero degree, pregnant with all past and future specifications. The word here has a generic form; it is a category. Each poetic word is thus an unexpected object, a Pandora's box from which fly out all the potentialities of language; it is therefore produced and consumed with a peculiar curiosity, a kind of sacred relish. This Hunger of the Word, common to the whole of modern poetry, makes poetic speech terrible and inhuman. It initiates a discourse full of gaps and full of lights, filled with absences and over-nourishing signs, without foresight or stability of intention, and thereby so opposed to the social function of language that merely to have recourse to a discontinuous speech is to open the door to all that stands above Nature.

For what does the rational economy of classical language mean, if not that Nature is a plenum, that it can be possessed, that it does not shy away or cover itself in shadows, but is in its entirety subjected to the toils of language? Classical language is always reducible to a persuasive continuum, it postulates the possibility of dialogue, it establishes a universe in which men are not alone, where words never have the terrible weight of things, where speech is always a meeting with the others. Classical language is a bringer of euphoria because it is immediately social. There is no genre, no written work of classicism which does not suppose a collective consumption, akin to speech; classical literary art is an object which circulates among several persons brought together on a class basis; it is a product conceived for oral transmission, for a consumption regulated by the contingencies of society: it is essentially a spoken language, in spite of its strict codification.

We have seen that on the contrary modern poetry destroyed relationships in language and reduced discourse to words as static things. This implies a reversal in our knowledge of Nature. The interrupted flow of the new poetic language initiates a discontinuous Nature, which is revealed only piecemeal. At the very moment when the withdrawal of functions obscures the relations existing in the world, the object in discourse assumes an exalted place : modern poetry is a poetry of the object. In it, Nature becomes a fragmented space, made of objects solitary and terrible, because the links between them are only potential. Nobody chooses for them a privileged meaning, or a particular use, or some service; nobody imposes a hierarchy on them, nobody reduces them to the manifestation of a mental behaviour, or of an intention, of some evidence of tenderness, in short. The bursting upon us of the poetic word then institutes an absolute object; Nature becomes a succession of verticalities, of objects, suddenly standing erect, and filled with all their possibilities : one of these can be only a landmark in an unfulfilled, and thereby terrible, world. These unrelated objects – words adorned with all the violence of their irruption, the vibration of which, though wholly mechanical, strangely affects the next word, only to die out immediately – these poetic words exclude men : there is no humanism of modern poetry. This erect discourse is full of terror, that is to say, it relates man not to other men, but to the most inhuman images in Nature : heaven, hell, holiness, childhood, madness, pure matter, etc.

At such a point, it is hardly possible to speak of a poetic mode of writing, for this is a language in which a violent drive towards autonomy destroys any ethical scope. The verbal gesture here aims at modifying Nature, it is the approach of a demiurge; it is not an attitude of the conscience but an act of coercion. Such, at least, is the language of those modern poets who carry their intention to the limit, and assume Poetry not as a spiritual exercise, a state of the soul or a placing of oneself in a situation, but as the splendour and freshness of a dream language. For such poets, it is as vain to speak about a mode of writing as of poetic feeling. Modern Poetry, in Char, for instance, is beyond this diffuse tone, this precious *aura*, which *are*, indeed, a mode of writing, usually termed poetic feeling. There is no objection to speaking of a poetic mode of writing concerning the classical writers and their epigones, or even concerning poetic prose in the manner of Gide's *Fruits of the Earth*, in which Poetry is in fact a certain linguistic ethos. In both cases, the mode of writing soaks up the style, and we can imagine that for people living in the seventeenth century, it was not easy to perceive an *immediate* difference between Racine and Pradon (and even less a difference of a poetic kind), just as it is not easy for a modern reader to pass judgment on those contemporary poets who use the same uniform and indecisive poetic mode of writing, because for them Poetry is a *climate* which means, essentially, a linguistic convention. But when the poetic language radically questions Nature by virtue of its very struc-

51

ture, without any resort to the content of the discourse and without falling back on some ideology, there is no mode of writing left, there are only styles, thanks to which man turns his back on society and confronts the world of objects without going through any of the forms of History or of social life.

Part Two

THE TRIUMPH AND BREAK-UP
OF BOURGEOIS WRITING

There is, in pre-classical Literature, the appearance of a variety of modes of writing; but this variety seems far less wide if one puts these linguistic problems in terms of structure and not in terms of art. Aesthetically, the sixteenth and the beginning of the seventeenth centuries show a fairly lavish profusion of literary languages because men are still engaged in the task of getting to know Nature, and not yet in that of giving expression to man's essence. On these grounds, the encyclopaedic writing of Rabelais, or the precious writing of Corneille – to take only such typical moments – have as a common form a language in which ornaments are not yet ritualistic but are in themselves a method of investigation applied to the whole surface of the world. This is what gives to this pre-classical writing the genuine appearance of many-sidedness, and the euphoria which comes from freedom. For a modern reader, the impression of variety is all the stronger since the French tongue seems to be still experimenting with unstable structures, and since it has not yet fully settled on the character of its syntax or the laws governing the increase of its vocabulary. To take up again the distinction between a language and a mode of writing, we can say that until around 1650, French literature had not yet gone further than the problematics of the language, and that by this very fact, it was as yet unaware of modes of writing. For as long as a tongue is still uncertain about its very structure, an ethics of language is impossible; modes of writing appear only when the language, being established on a national scale, becomes a kind of negativity, a line which separates what is forbidden from what is allowed, without asking itself any more questions about its origins or the justifications for such a taboo. By creating an intemporal reason working through the language, the classical grammarians have relieved the French from any linguistic problem, and this purified language has become a mode of writing, that is, a language to which is attached a value, and which is given immediately as universal by very virtue of the historical situation.

The diversity of the 'genres' and the varying rhythms of styles within the framework of classical dogma are aesthetic, not structural, data; neither must deceive us: there was indeed one and only one mode of writing, both instrumental and ornamental, at the disposal of French society during the whole period when bourgeois ideology conquered and triumphed. Instrumental, since form was supposed to be at the service of content, just as an algebraic equation is at the service of an operational process; ornamental, since the instrument in question was embellished with accidental features external to its function, and unselfconsciously borrowed from Tradition, so that this bourgeois mode of writing, taken in turn by different writers, was never shunned for its pedigree, since it was only a felicitous backcloth against which the act of thought was thrown into relief. Classical writers have indeed themselves faced problems of form, but the point at issue was in no way the plurality and meaning of modes of writing, still less the structure of the language. The only thing in question was rhetoric, namely the ordering of discourse in such a way as to persuade. To a single bourgeois writing there corresponded, therefore, several rhetorics; conversely, it was at the very moment when treatises on rhetoric aroused no more interest, towards the middle of the nineteenth century, that classical writing ceased to be universal and that modern modes of writing came into being.

This classical writing is, needless to say, a class writing. Born in the seventeenth century in the group which was closest to the people in power, shaped by force of dogmatic decisions, promptly ridding itself of all grammatical turns of speech forged by the spontaneous subjectivity of ordinary people, and drilled, on the contrary, for a task of definition, bourgeois writing was first presented, with the cynicism

customary in the first flush of political victory, as
the language of a privileged minority. In 1647,
Vaugelas recommends classical writing as a *de facto*,
not a *de jure*, state of affairs; clear expression is still
only court usage. In 1660, on the contrary, in the
Grammaire of Port-Royal for instance, classical language wears a universal look, and clarity has become
a value. In actual fact, clarity is a purely rhetorical
attribute, not a quality of language in general, which
is possible at all times and in all places, but only the
ideal appendage to a certain type of discourse, that
which is given over to a permanent intention to persuade. It is because the pre-bourgeoisie of the *Ancien
Régime* and the post-revolutionary bourgeoisie, using
the same mode of writing, have developed an essen-
tialist mythology of man, that classical writing, unified and universal, renounced all hesitancy in favour
of a continuum in which every fragment was a
choice, that is, the radical elimination of all virtuali-
ties in language. Political authority, spiritualistic
dogmatism, and unity in the language of classicism
are therefore various aspects of the same historical
movement.

So it is no wonder that the Revolution changed
nothing in bourgeois writing, and that there is only a
slight difference between the writing of, say, Fénelon
and Mérimée. This is because bourgeois ideology remained intact until 1848 without being in the least
shaken by a Revolution which gave the bourgeoisie

political and social power, although not the intellectual power, which it had long held. From Laclos to
Stendhal, bourgeois writing needed only to resume its
continuity after the short interruption of troubled
times. And the romantic revolution, so theoretically
committed to the overthrow of traditional forms, in
the event, stuck prudently to the writing of its ideology. A few concessions such as the mixing of genres
and words enabled it to preserve the main feature of
classical language, namely, instrumentality. True, this
instrument comes more and more to the fore (notably
in Chateaubriand), but all in all it is still an instrument, used without aloofness, and not yet, as a language, conscious of solitude. Hugo alone, by evolving,
out of the concrete dimensions of his own personal
time and space, a particular and thematic use of language, which could no longer be understood with
reference to a tradition, but only in the light of the
formidable reality lying behind his own existence,
Hugo alone, then, through the weight of his style,
was able to exert some pressure on classical writing
and bring it to the verge of disintegration. This is
why contempt for Hugo still serves to bolster up the
self-same writing in eighteenth century taste, which
witnessed the heyday of the bourgeoisie, and remains
the norm of 'accepted' French, a carefully closed language, separated from society by the whole body of
the literary myth, a consecrated mode of writing used
indiscriminately by the most heterogeneous writers as

an austere duty or a connoisseur's relish, a tabernacle of this awe-inspiring mystery: French Literature.

Now the 1850s bring the concurrence of three new and important facts in History: the demographic expansion in Europe, the replacement of textile by heavy industry, that is, the birth of modern capitalism, the scission (completed by the revolution of June 1848) of French society into three mutually hostile classes, bringing the definitive ruin of liberal illusions. These circumstances put the bourgeoisie into a new historical situation. Until then, it was bourgeois ideology itself which gave the measure of the universal by fulfilling it unchallenged. The bourgeois writer, sole judge of other people's woes and without anyone else to gaze on him, was not torn between his social condition and his intellectual vocation. Henceforth, this very ideology appears merely as one among many possible others; the universal escapes it, since transcending itself would mean condemning itself; the writer falls a prey to ambiguity, since his consciousness no longer accounts for the whole of his condition. Thus is born a tragic predicament peculiar to Literature.

It is at this moment that modes of writing begin to multiply. Each one, henceforth, be it the highly wrought, populist, neutral or colloquial, sets itself up as the initial act whereby the writer acknowledges or repudiates his bourgeois condition. Each one is an attempt to find a solution to this Orphean problematics of modern Form : writers without Literature. For the last hundred years, Flaubert, Mallarmé, Rimbaud, the Goncourt brothers, the Surrealists, Queneau, Sartre, Blanchot or Camus, have outlined – indeed are still outlining – certain ways of integrating, disrupting or naturalizing literary language; but what is at stake is not some adventure of literary form, some success in rhetorical achievement or some bold use of vocabulary. Whenever the writer assembles a network of words it is the existence of Literature itself which is called into question; what modernity allows us to read in the plurality of modes of writing, is the blind alley which is its own History.

STYLE AS CRAFTSMANSHIP

'Form is costly,' Valéry would answer when asked
why he did not publish his lectures at the Collège de
France. Yet there has been a whole period, that of
triumphant bourgeois writing, when form cost about
the same price as thought. It is true that attention
was paid to its conciseness and order, and to its
euphemistic grace, but form was all the cheaper since
the writer was using a ready-made instrument, the
working of which was handed down unchanged
without anyone being obsessed with novelty. Form
was not seen as a possession; the universality of
classical language derived from the fact that language
was common property, and that thought alone bore
the weight of being different. We might say that
throughout this period, form had a usage value.

Now we have seen that around 1850, Literature begins to face a problem of self-justification; it is now
on the point of seeking alibis for itself; and precisely
because the shadow of a doubt begins to be cast on its
usage, a whole class of writers anxious to assume to
the full the responsibility of their tradition is about to
put the work-value of writing in place of its usage-

value. Writing is now to be saved not by virtue of what it exists for, but thanks to the work it has cost. There begins now to grow up an image of the writer as a craftsman who shuts himself away in some legendary place, like a workman operating at home, and who roughs out, cuts, polishes and sets his form exactly as a jeweller extracts art from his material, devoting to his work regular hours of solitary effort. Writers like Gautier (past master in Belles-Lettres), Flaubert (grinding away at his sentences at Croisset), Valéry (in his room at the crack of dawn) or Gide (standing at his desk like a carpenter at his bench) form a kind of guild of French Literature, in which work expended on form is the sign and the property of a corporation. Labour replaces genius as a value, so to speak; there is a kind of ostentation in claiming to labour long and lovingly over the form of one's work. There even arises, sometimes, a preciosity of conciseness (for labouring at one's material usually means reducing it), in contrast to the great preciosity of the baroque era (that of Corneille, for instance). For the latter expresses a knowledge of Nature which necessitates a broadening of the language; but the former, trying to evolve an aristocratic literary style, lays down the conditions for a historical crisis, destined to begin on the day when an aesthetic aim no longer suffices to justify the convention which this anachronistic language represents, that is, on the day when History has brought about an obvious disjunction between the social vocation of the writer and the instrument which he has inherited from Tradition.

Flaubert it was who most methodically laid the foundations for this conception of writing as craft. Before him, the existence of the bourgeois was a picturesque or exotic phenomenon; bourgeois ideology supplied the norm of the universal and, postulating that pure man existed as such, could experience a sense of well-being as it contemplated the bourgeois as a spectacle in no way commensurate with itself. Whereas for Flaubert the bourgeois state is an incurable ill which sticks to the writer, and which he can cure only by assuming it clear-sightedly – which is of the essence of tragic feeling. This bourgeois Necessity which characterizes Frédéric Moreau, Emma Bovary, Bouvard and Pécuchet, requires, as soon as it is squarely faced and accepted, an art which is equally the bearer of a necessity, and armed with a Law. Flaubert founded a normative writing which – and this is a paradox – includes technical rules which can reveal pathos. On the one hand, he builds his narrative by a succession of essences, and not at all by following a phenomenological order (as Proust later does); he finalizes the uses of verbal tenses according to a convention, so as to make them perform the function of *signs* of Literature, in the manner of an art drawing attention to its very artificiality; he elaborates a rhythm of the written word which creates a sort of incantation and which, quite unlike the rules of spoken eloquence, appeals to a sixth, purely literary, sense, the private property of producers and consumers of Literature. And on the other hand this code of literary labour, this sum of exercises related to the writer's work, keep up a wisdom, so to speak, which is also touched with sadness, and openness too, since the art of Flaubert points to its mask as it moves forward. What this Gregorian codification of literary language aimed at was, if not the reconciliation of the writer to a universal condition, at least the conferment upon him of the responsibility for his form, the transmutation of the writing handed down to him by History into an *art*, in other words, into an obvious convention, a sincere pact which would enable man to adopt a position he was familiar with in a nature still made of ill-matched realities. The writer then gives to society a self-confessed art, whose rules are visible to all, and in exchange society is able to accept the writer. Baudelaire, for instance, insisted on tracing the admirable prosaicness of his poetry back to Gautier, to a kind of fetish of *highly wrought* form, situated no doubt outside pragmatic bourgeois activity, but inserted into an order of familiar tasks, under the eye of a society which recognized in it not its dreams but its methods. Since Literature could not be vanquished by its own weapons, was it not better to accept it openly, and, being condemned to this literary hard labour, to 'do good work' in it? So the 'Flaubertization' of writing redeems all writers at a stroke, partly because the least exacting abandon themselves to it without qualms, and partly because the purest return to it as to an acknowledgment of their fate.

WRITING AND REVOLUTION

The conception of style as craftsmanship has produced a mode of sub-writing, derived from Flaubert, but adapted to the aims of the Naturalist school. This writing, which is that of Maupassant, Zola and Daudet and which could be called the realist mode of writing, is a combination of the formal signs of Literature (preterite, indirect speech, the rhythm of written language) and of the no less formal signs of realism (incongruous snippets of popular speech, strong language or dialect words, etc.), so that no mode of writing was more artificial than that which set out to give the most accurate description of Nature. This is no mere stylistic failure but one of theory as well: there is, in the Naturalist aesthetic, a convention of the real, just as there is a fabrication in its writing. The paradox is that the abasement of subjects has not in the least entailed the unobtrusiveness of form. Neutral writing is a late phenomenon to be invented only much later than Realism by authors like Camus, less under the impulse of an aesthetics of escape than in search of a mode of writing which might at last achieve innocence. The writing of Realism is far from being neutral, it is on the contrary loaded with the most spectacular signs of fabrication.

Thus, when it became degraded by abandoning the insistence on a verbal Nature openly foreign to reality, while still not pretending to revert to the language of social Nature – as did Queneau later – the Naturalist school paradoxically evolved a mechanical art which flaunted the signs of literary convention with an ostentation hitherto unknown. In Flaubertian writing a spell was gradually woven, and it is still possible to lose oneself reading Flaubert as if one were in a nature full of echoing voices in which signs are rather persuasive than expressive. Whereas the writing of Realism can never be convincing; it is condemned to mere description by virtue of this dualistic dogma which ordains that there shall only ever be one optimum form to 'express' a reality as inert as an object, on which the writer can have no power except through his art of arranging the signs.

These authors without a style – Maupassant, Zola, Daudet and their epigones – have used a mode of writing which represented for them a means both of rescuing and displaying the craftsmanship which they fancied they had expelled from a purely passive aesthetic. Maupassant's declarations on the labour associated with form are well known, as are all the naive devices of his school, whereby the natural sentence is transformed into an artificial one meant to bear witness to its purely literary purpose, which means, in this instance, to what it cost in labour. We know that according to Maupassant's stylistics, the artistic intention is the preserve of syntax, the vocabulary being meant to stay on this side of Literature. To write well – now the sole sign of literary reality – means naively to shift the place of a predicate, to 'set off' a word while being hopeful of obtaining by this means an 'expressive' rhythm. But expressiveness is a myth: it is only the convention of expressiveness.

This conventional mode of writing has always been a happy hunting ground for study in schools, where the value of a text is assessed by the obvious signs of the labour it has cost. Now nothing is more spectacular than attempting to combine predicates, as a workman adjusts some delicate mechanism. What pedants admire in the writing of a Maupassant or a Daudet is a literary sign at last detached from its content, which posits Literature unambiguously as a category without any relation to other languages, and 'in so doing establishes an ideal intelligibility of things. Between a proletariat excluded from all culture, and an intelligentsia which has already begun to question Literature itself, the average public produced by primary and secondary schools, namely lower-middle class, roughly speaking, will therefore find in the artistic-realistic mode of writing – which is that of a good proportion of commercial novels – the image *par excellence* of a Literature which has all the striking and intelligible signs of its identity. In this case the function of the writer is not so much to create a work as to supply a Literature which can be seen from afar.

This lower-middle-class mode of writing has been taken up by communist writers because, for the time being, the artistic norms of the proletariat cannot be different from those of the *petite bourgeoisie* (a fact which indeed agrees with their doctrine), and because the very dogma of socialist realism necessarily entails the adoption of a conventional mode of writing, to which is assigned the task of signifying in a conspicuous way a content which is powerless to impose itself without a form to identify it. Thus is understood the paradox whereby the communist mode of writing makes multiple use of the grossest signs of Literature, and far from breaking with a form which is after all typically bourgeois – or which was such in the past, at least – goes on assuming without reservation the formal preoccupations of the *petit-bourgeois* art of writing (which is moreover accredited with the communist public, thanks to the essays done in the primary school).

French socialist realism has therefore taken up the mode of writing of bourgeois realism, mechanizing without restraint all the intentional signs of art. Here are for instance a few lines of a novel by Garaudy:
' ... with torso bent, he launched himself at full speed on the keyboard of the linotype ... joy sang in his muscles, his fingers danced, light and powerful ... the poisoned vapour of antimony ... made his temples pulsate and his arteries hammer, fanning his strength, his anger and his mental exaltation.' We see that nothing here is given without metaphor, for it must be laboriously borne home to the reader that 'it is well written' (that is, that what he is consuming is Literature). These metaphors, which seize the very slightest verb, in no way indicate the intention of an individual Humour trying to convey the singularity of a sensation, but only a literary stamp which 'places' a language, just as a label tells us the price of an article.

'To type', 'to throb' or 'to be happy for the first time', is real, not Realist language; for Literature to come into existence one must write: 'to strum on the linotype', 'his arteries hammered ... ' or 'he was clutching the first happy moment of his life.' Realist writing can therefore lead only to a species of preciosity. Garaudy writes: 'At the end of each line, the thin arm of the linotype plucked away a handful of dancing matrices,' or 'Each caress of his fingers awakes and sends a shiver through the joyous chime of copper matrices which fall into the grooves in a tinkling shower of notes.' This jargon is really no different from that of Cathos and Magdelon.*

Of course, we must allow for mediocrity; in the case of Garaudy, it is impressive. In André Stil, we shall find devices which are much more discreet but which do not escape the rules of artistic-realist writing. Here metaphors do not pretend to be more than a cliché, almost fully integrated to real language, and signifying Literature at no great cost: 'crystal clear', 'hands white as parchment with the cold', etc. The preciosity is driven from the vocabulary into the syntax, and it is the artificial arrangement of the predicates, as in Maupassant, which establishes the text as Literature ('with one hand, she lifts up the knees, her body bent'). This language, steeped in conventionality, presents reality only in inverted commas: would-be working-class words, slipshod turns of speech are used together with a purely literary syntax: 'That's true, it's kicking up a shindy all right, that wind!', or even better: 'Their bérets and caps buffeted in the wind above their eyes, they look at each other pretty quizzically' (in which the colloquial 'pretty' follows an absolute participle, a form of speech totally unknown in spoken language). Needless to say, one must set Aragon in a class apart, since his literary antecedents are of a quite different kind, and since he has preferred to mix in with realist writing a slight

* Cathos and Magdelon are Molière's *Précieuses Ridicules*.

eighteenth century colour, adding a little Laclos to Zola.

Perhaps there is, in this well-behaved writing of revolutionaries, a feeling of powerlessness to create forthwith a free writing. Perhaps also the fact that only bourgeois writers can feel that bourgeois writing is compromised: the disintegration of literary language was a phenomenon which owed its existence to consciousness, not to revolution. And certainly the fact that Stalinist ideology imposes a terror before all problematics, even and above all revolutionary: bourgeois writing is thought to be all in all less dangerous than its being put on trial. This is why communist writers are the only ones who go on imperturbably keeping alive a bourgeois writing which bourgeois writers have themselves condemned long ago, since the day when they felt it was endangered by the impostures of their own ideology, namely, the day when Marxism was thereby justified.

WRITING AND SILENCE

Craftsmanlike writing, since it lies within the bourgeois heritage, does not disturb any order; although deprived of other battles, the writer retains a passion which provides him with sufficient justification: the bringing forth of form. If he renounces the task of setting free a new literary language, he can at least enhance the existing one with new intentions, conceits, purple patches or archaisms, and create another, which is rich and mortal. This great traditional writing, that of Gide, Valéry, Montherlant, even Breton, means that form, through the weight of its unusual posturing, is a value which transcends History, in the same way as a ritual language of priests.

Other writers have thought that they could exorcize this sacred writing only by dislocating it. They have therefore undermined literary language, they have ceaselessly exploded the ever-renewed husk of clichés, of habits, of the formal past of the writer; in a chaos of forms and a wilderness of words they hoped they would achieve an object wholly delivered of History, and find again the freshness of a pristine state of language. But such upheavals end up by leaving their own tracks and creating their own laws. The threat of becoming a Fine Art is a fate which hangs over any language not based exclusively on the speech of society. In a perpetual flight forward from a disorderly syntax, the disintegration of language can only lead to the silence of writing. The final agraphia of Rimbaud or of some Surrealists (who *ipso facto* fell into oblivion), this poignant self-destruction of Literature, teaches us that for some writers, language, the first and last way out of the literary myth, finally restores what it had hoped to avoid, that there is no writing which can be lastingly revolutionary, and that any silence of form can escape imposture only by complete abandonment of communication. Mallarmé, the Hamlet of writing, as it were, well represents this precarious moment of History in which literary language persists only the better to sing the necessity of its death. Mallarmé's typographical agraphia seeks to create around rarefied words an empty zone in which speech, liberated from its guilty social overtones, may, by some happy contrivance, no longer reverberate. The word, dissociated from the husk of habitual clichés, and from the technical reflexes of the writer, is then freed from responsibility in relation to all possible context; it appears in one brief act, which, being devoid of reflections, declares its solitude, and therefore its innocence. This art has the very structure of suicide: in it, silence is a homogeneous poetic time which traps the word between two layers and sets it off less as a fragment of a cryptogram than as a light, a void, a murder, a freedom. (We know all that this hypothesis of Mallarmé as a murderer of language owes to Maurice Blanchot.) This language of Mallarmé's is like Orpheus who can save what he loves only by renouncing it, and who, just the same, cannot resist glancing round a little; it is Literature brought to the gates of the Promised Land: a world without Literature, but one to which writers would nevertheless have to bear witness.

In this same attempt towards disengaging literary language, here is another solution: to create a colourless writing, freed from all bondage to a pre-ordained state of language. A simile borrowed from linguistics will perhaps give a fairly accurate idea of this new phenomenon; we know that some linguists establish between the two terms of a polar opposition (such as singular-plural, preterite-present) the existence of a third term, called a neutral term or zero element: thus between the subjunctive and the imperative moods, the indicative is according to them an amodal form. Proportionately speaking, writing at the zero degree is basically in the indicative mood, or if you like, amodal; it would be accurate to say that it is a journalist's writing, if it were not precisely the case that journalism develops, in general, optative or imperative (that is, emotive) forms. The new neutral writing takes its place in the midst of all those ejaculations and judgments, without becoming involved in any of them; it consists precisely in their absence. But this absence is complete, it implies no refuge, no secret; one cannot therefore say that it is an impassive mode of writing; rather, that it is innocent. The aim here is to go beyond Literature by entrusting one's fate to a sort of basic speech, equally far from living languages and from literary language proper. This transparent form of speech, initiated by Camus's *Outsider*, achieves a style of absence which is almost an ideal absence of style; writing is then reduced to a sort of negative mood in which the social or mythical characters of a language are abolished in favour of a neutral and inert state of form; thus thought remains wholly responsible, without being overlaid by a secondary commitment of form to a History not its own. If Flaubert's writing enshrines a Law, if that of Mallarmé postulates a silence, and if others, those of Proust, Céline, Queneau, Prévert, each in its own way, is founded on the existence of a social nature, if all these modes of writing imply an opacity of form and presuppose a problematic of language and society, thus establishing speech as an object which must receive treatment at the hands of a craftsman, a magician or a scriptor, but not by an intellectual, then neutral writing in fact rediscovers the primary

77

condition of classical art: instrumentality. But this time, form as an instrument is no longer at the service of a triumphant ideology; it is the mode of a new situation of the writer, the way a certain silence has of existing; it deliberately forgoes any elegance or ornament, for these two dimensions would reintroduce Time into writing, and this is a derivative power which sustains History. If the writing is really neutral, and if language, instead of being a cumbersome and recalcitrant act, reaches the state of a pure equation, which is no more tangible than an algebra when it confronts the innermost part of man, then Literature is vanquished, the problematics of mankind is uncovered and presented without elaboration, the writer becomes irretrievably honest. Unfortunately, nothing is more fickle than a colourless writing; mechanical habits are developed in the very place where freedom existed, a network of set forms hem in more and more the pristine freshness of discourse, a mode of writing appears afresh in lieu of an indefinite language. The writer, taking his place as a 'classic', becomes the slavish imitator of his original creation, society demotes his writing to a mere manner, and returns him a prisoner to his own formal myths.

WRITING AND SPEECH

A little more than a hundred years ago, writers were for the most part unaware that there were several ways – and very different ones – of speaking French. Around 1830, at the time when the bourgeoisie found good-humoured entertainment in everything situated on the fringe of its own preserve, namely in that inconsiderable portion of society which it was willing to share with bohemians, concierges and pickpockets, there began to find their way into literary language proper a few extraneous scraps lifted from inferior forms of language, provided they were suitably eccentric (otherwise they would have been a source of danger). These picturesque jargons embellished Literature without threatening its structure. Balzac, Süe, Monnier, Hugo found enjoyment in reinstating a few really aberrant forms of pronunciation and vocabulary: thieves' argot, country dialects, German jargon, or the lingo of the concierges. But this social speech, which was a kind of theatrical costume hung on to an essence, never involved the speaker as a total person; the mechanism of the passions went on functioning over and above the speech.

It was perhaps necessary to wait for Proust to see the writer fuse certain men totally with their language, and present his creatures only through that solid and colourful guise, their way of speaking. While Balzac's creatures, for instance, are easily reducible to the power relations of the society of which they are, so to speak, the algebraic expressions, a character of Proust materializes into the opacity of a particular language, and it is really at this level that his whole historical situation – his profession, his class, his wealth, his heredity, his bodily frame – is integrated and ordered. In this way, Literature begins to know society as a Nature, the phenomena of which it might perhaps be able to reproduce. During such moments when the writer follows languages which are really spoken, no longer for the sake of picturesqueness, but as essential objects which fully account for the whole content of society, writing takes as the locus of its reflexes the real speech of men. Literature no longer implies pride or escape, it begins to become a lucid act of giving information; as if it had first to learn the particulars of social differences by reproducing them. It takes it upon itself to give an immediate account, as a preliminary to any other message, of the situation of men immured by the language of their class, their region, their profession, their heredity or their history.

Understood in this way, literary language founded on social speech never gets rid of a descriptive virtue

which limits it, since the universality of a language –
in the present state of society – is a fact concerning
hearing, and not speaking. Within a national norm
such as French, forms of expression differ in different
groups, and every man is a prisoner of his language:
outside his class, the first word he speaks is a sign
which places him as a whole and proclaims his whole
personal history. The man is put on show and delivered up by his language, betrayed by a formal
reality which is beyond the reach of his lies, whether
they are inspired by self-interest or generosity. The
diversity of languages therefore works like Necessity,
and it is because of this that it gives rise to a form of
the tragic.

So the restoration of spoken language, first invented in the playful mimicry of the picturesque,
ended by expressing the whole content of social contradiction. In Céline's work, for instance, writing is
not at the service of thought, like some successfully
realistic décor tacked on to the description of a social
sub-class; it really represents the writer's descent into
the sticky opacity of the condition which he is describing. True, this is still a way of *expressing* it, and
Literature has not been left behind. But it must be
agreed that, among all the means of *description* (since
until now Literature has above all aimed at that), the

adoption of a real language is for the writer the most human act. And a sizable part of modern Literature is pervaded by the more or less elaborate shreds of this dream: a literary language which might emulate the naturalness of social languages. (We have only to think of the dialogues in Sartre's novels to give a recent and well-known example.) But however successful these pictures may be, they can never be any more than reproductions, arias, so to speak, surrounded by long recitatives in an entirely conventional mode of writing.

Queneau has tried, precisely, to show that it was possible to contaminate all the parts of the written discourse by spoken speech, and in his works the socialization of literary language takes a simultaneous hold on all the layers of writing: the spelling, the vocabulary, and – which is more important although less spectacular – the pace. Of course, this writing of Queneau's is not situated outside Literature, since it is still consumed by a limited section of society; it is not the vehicle of a universality, but only of an experiment and an entertainment. At least, for the first time, it is not the writing which is literary; Literature is expelled from Form and is now nothing but a category. Here, it is Literature which is irony, and language which is experienced in depth. Or rather, Literature is openly reduced to the problematics of language; and indeed, that is all it can now be.

We can see taking shape, by this means, the possible area of a new humanism: the general suspicion which has gradually overtaken language throughout modern literature gives way to a reconciliation between the logos of the writer and that of men. Only then can the writer declare himself entirely committed, when his poetic freedom takes its place within a verbal condition whose limits are those of society and not those of a convention or a public. Otherwise, commitment will always be purely nominal; it will be able to effect the salvation of one conscience, but not to provide a basis for action. It is because there is no thought without language, that Form is the first and last arbiter of literary responsibility, and it is because there is no reconciliation within the present society, that language, necessary and necessarily orientated, creates for the writer a situation fraught with conflict.

THE UTOPIA OF LANGUAGE

The multiplication of modes of writing is a modern phenomenon which forces a choice upon the writer, making form a kind of behaviour and giving rise to an ethic of writing. To all the dimensions which together made up the literary creation is henceforth added a new depth, since form is by itself a kind of parasitical mechanism of the intellectual function. Modern writing is a truly independent organism which grows around the literary act, decorates it with a value which is foreign to its intention, ceaselessly commits it to a double mode of existence, and superimposes upon the content of the words opaque signs which carry with them a history, a second-order meaning which compromises or redeems it, so that with the situation of thought is mingled a supplementary fate, often diverging from the former and always an encumbrance to it – the fate of the form.

Now this fatal character of the literary sign, which makes a writer unable to pen a word without taking a pose characteristic of an out-of-date, anarchic or imitative language – one in any case conventionalized and dehumanized – has taken effect precisely at the moment when Literature, abolishing more and more its condition as a bourgeois myth, is required as a document or a testimony of a humanism which has at last integrated History into its image of man. So that the old literary categories, emptied in the best instances of their traditional content, which was the expression of an intemporal essence of man, eventually stand only by virtue of a specific form, an order due to the vocabulary or the syntax, in short, quite simply a language: it is now writing which absorbs the whole identity of a literary work. A novel by Sartre is a novel only to the extent of its having remained faithful to a certain recitative tone, which is, moreover, intermittent, and whose norms have been established in the course of a whole previous geology of the novel: in fact, it is the mode of writing of the recitative, and not its content, which reintegrates the Sartrean novel into the category of Belles-Lettres. Furthermore, when Sartre attempts to break the time-flow typical of the novel, and duplicates his narrative in order to render the ubiquity of reality (in *The Reprieve*), it is the narrative mode of writing which recomposes, above the simultaneity of the events, a Time which is undivided and homogeneous, the Time of the Narrator, whose particular voice, defined by highly recognizable contingent features, burdens the unfolding of History with a parasitical unity, and gives the novel the ambiguity of a testimony which may well be false.

This shows that a modern masterpiece is impossible, since the writer is forced by his writing into a cleft stick: either the object of the work is naively attuned to the conventions of its form, Literature remaining deaf to our present History, and not going beyond the literary myth; or else the writer acknowledges the vast novelty of the present world, but finds that in order to express it he has at his disposal only a language which is splendid but lifeless. In front of the virgin sheet of paper, at the moment of choosing the words which must frankly signify his place in History, and testify that he assumes its data, he observes a tragic disparity between what he does and what he sees. Before his eyes, the world of society now exists as a veritable Nature, and this Nature speaks, elaborating living languages from which the writer is excluded: on the contrary, History puts in his hands a decorative and compromising instrument, a writing inherited from a previous and different History, for which he is not responsible and yet which is the only one he can use. Thus is born a tragic element in writing, since the conscious writer must henceforth fight against ancestral and all-powerful signs which, from the depths of a past foreign to him, impose Literature on him like some ritual, not like a reconciliation.

Therefore, unless they renounced Literature, the solution of this problematic of writing does not depend on the writer. Every writer born opens within himself the trial of literature, but if he condemns it, he always grants it a reprieve which literature turns to use in order to reconquer him. However hard he tries to create a free language, it comes back to him fabricated, for luxury is never innocent: and it is this stale language, closed by the immense pressure of all the men who do not speak it, which he must continue to use. Writing therefore is a blind alley, and it is because society itself is a blind alley. The writers of today feel this; for them, the search for a non-style or an oral style, for a zero level or a spoken level of writing is, all things considered, the anticipation of a homogeneous social state; most of them understand that there can be no universal language outside a concrete, and no longer a mystical or merely nominal, universality of society.

There is therefore in every present mode of writing a double postulation: there is the impetus of a break and the impetus of a coming to power, there is the very shape of every revolutionary situation, the fundamental ambiguity of which is that Revolution must of necessity borrow, from what it wants to destroy, the very image of what it wants to possess. Like modern art in its entirety, literary writing carries at the same time the alienation of History and the dream of History; as a Necessity, it testifies to the division of languages which is inseparable from the division of classes; as Freedom, it is the consciousness of this division and the very effort which seeks to surmount it. Feeling permanently guilty of its own solitude, it is none the less an imagination eagerly desiring a felicity of words, it hastens towards a dreamed-of language whose freshness, by a kind of ideal anticipation, might portray the perfection of some new Adamic world where language would no longer be alienated. The proliferation of modes of writing brings a new Literature into being in so far as the latter invents its language only in order to be a project: Literature becomes the Utopia of language.

Elements of Semiology

Contents

INTRODUCTION

In his *Course in General Linguistics,* first published in 1916, Saussure postulated the existence of a general science of signs, or Semiology, of which linguistics would form only one part. Semiology therefore aims to take in any system of signs, whatever their substance and limits; images, gestures, musical sounds, objects, and the complex associations of all these, which form the content of ritual, convention or public entertainment: these constitute, if not *languages*, at least systems of signification. There is no doubt that the development of mass communications confers particular relevance today upon the vast field of signifying media, just when the success of disciplines such as linguistics, information theory, formal logic and structural anthropology provide semantic analysis with new instruments. There is at present a kind of demand for semiology, stemming not from the fads of a few scholars, but from the very history of the modern world.

The fact remains that, although Saussure's ideas have made great headway, semiology remains a tentative science. The reason for this may well be simple. Saussure, followed in this by the main semiologists, thought that linguistics merely formed a part of the general science of signs. Now it is far from certain that in the social life of today there are to be found any extensive systems of signs outside human language. Semiology has so far concerned itself with codes of no more than slight interest, such as the Highway Code; the moment we go on to systems where the sociological significance is more than superficial, we are once more confronted with language. It is true that objects, images and patterns of behaviour can signify, and do so on a large scale, but never autonomously; every semiological system has its linguistic admixture. Where there is a visual substance, for example, the meaning is confirmed by being duplicated in a linguistic message (which happens in the case of the cinema, advertising, comic strips, press photography, etc.) so that at least a part of the iconic message is, in terms of structural relationship, either redundant or taken up by the linguistic system. As for collections of objects (clothes, food), they enjoy the status of systems only in so far as they pass through the relay of language, which extracts their signifiers (in the form of nomenclature) and names their signifieds* (in the forms of usages or reasons): we are, much more than in former times, and despite the spread of pictorial illustration, a civilization of the written word. Finally, and in more general terms, it appears increasingly more difficult to conceive a system of images and objects whose *signifieds* can exist independently of language: to perceive what a substance signifies is inevitably to fall back on the individuation of a language: there is no meaning which is not designated, and the world of signifieds is none other than that of language.

Thus, though working at the outset on non-linguistic substances, semiology is required, sooner or later, to find language (in the ordinary sense of the

---

* We have preferred English to Latin in translating *signifiant* and *signifié*, even at the cost of the inelegant plural 'signifieds'.

term) in its path, not only as a model, but also as component, relay or signified. Even so, such language is not quite that of the linguist: it is a second-order language, with its unities no longer monemes or phonemes, but larger fragments of discourse referring to objects or episodes whose meaning *underlies* language, but can never exist independently of it. Semiology is therefore perhaps destined to be absorbed into a *trans-linguistics*, the materials of which may be myth, narrative, journalism, or on the other hand objects of our civilization, in so far as they are *spoken* (through press, prospectus, interview, conversation and perhaps even the inner language, which is ruled by the laws of imagination). In fact, we must now face the possibility of inverting Saussure's declaration: linguistics is not a part of the general science of signs, even a privileged part, it is semiology which is a part of linguistics: to be precise, it is that part covering the *great signifying unities* of discourse. By this inversion we may expect to bring to light the unity of the research at present being done in anthropology, sociology, psycho-analysis and stylistics round the concept of signification.

Though it will doubtless be required some day to change its character, semiology must first of all, if not exactly take definite shape, at least *try itself out*, explore its possibilities and impossibilities. This is feasible only on the basis of preparatory investigation. And indeed it must be acknowledged in advance that such an investigation is both diffident and rash: diffident because semiological knowledge at present can be only a copy of linguistic knowledge; rash because this knowledge must be applied forthwith, at least as a project, to non-linguistic objects.

INTRODUCTION

The *Elements* here presented have as their sole aim the extraction from linguistics of analytical concepts[1] which we think *a priori* to be sufficiently general to start semiological research on its way. In assembling them, it is not presupposed that they will remain intact during the course of research; nor that semiology will always be forced to follow the linguistic model closely.[2] We are merely suggesting and elucidating a terminology in the hope that it may enable an initial (albeit provisional) order to be introduced into the heterogeneous mass of significant facts. In fact what we purport to do is to furnish a principle of classification of the questions.

These elements of semiology will therefore be grouped under four main headings borrowed from structural linguistics:

I. *Language and Speech.*
II. *Signified and Signifier.*
III. *Syntagm and System.*
IV. *Denotation and Connotation.*

It will be seen that these headings appear in dichotomic form; the reader will also notice that the binary classification of concepts seems frequent in structural thought,[3] as if the metalanguage of the linguist reproduced, like a mirror, the binary structure of the system it is describing; and we shall point out, as the occasion arises, that it would probably be very instructive to study the pre-eminence of binary classification in the discourse of contemporary social sciences. The taxonomy of these sciences, if it were well known, would undoubtedly provide a great deal of information on what might be called the field of intellectual imagination in our time.

I. LANGUAGE (*LANGUE*) AND SPEECH

I.1. IN LINGUISTICS

I.1.1. *In Saussure:* The (dichotomic) concept of *language/speech* is central in Saussure* and was certainly a great novelty in relation to earlier linguistics which sought to find the causes of historical changes in the evolution of pronunciation, spontaneous associations and the working of analogy, and was therefore a linguistics of the individual act. In working out this famous dichotomy, Saussure started from the 'multiform and heterogeneous' nature of language, which appears at first sight as an unclassifiable reality[1] the unity of which cannot be brought to light, since it partakes at the same time of the physical, the physiological, the mental, the individual and the social. Now this disorder disappears if, from this heterogeneous whole, is extracted a purely social object, the systematized set of conventions necessary to communication, indifferent to the *material* of the signals which compose it, and which is a *language* (*langue*); as opposed to which *speech* (*parole*) covers the purely individual part of language (phonation, application of the rules and contingent combinations of signs).

* The Saussurean notions of *langue* and *parole* present to the translator into English notorious difficulties, which their

I.1.2. *The language* (*langue*): *A language* is therefore, so to speak, language minus speech: it is at the same time a social institution and a system of values. As a social institution, it is by no means an act, and it is not subject to any premeditation. It is the social part of language, the individual cannot by himself either create or modify it; it is essentially a collective contract which one must accept in its entirety if one wishes to communicate. Moreover, this social product is autonomous, like a game with its own rules, for it can be handled only after a period of learning. As a system of values, a language is made of a certain number of elements, each one of which is at the same time the equivalent of a given quantity of things and a term of a larger function, in which are found, in a differential order, other correlative values: from the point of view of the language, the sign is like a coin[5] which has the value of a certain amount of goods which it allows one to buy, but also has value in relation to other coins, in a greater or lesser degree. The institutional and the systematic aspect are of course connected: it is because a language is a system of contractual values (in part arbitrary, or, more exactly, unmotivated) that it resists the modifications coming from a single individual, and is consequently a social institution.

I.1.3. *Speech* (*parole*): In contrast to the language, which is both institution and system, *speech* is essen-

extension in the present work does nothing to alleviate. We have translated *langue* as 'a' or '*the* language', except when the coupling with 'speech' makes the meaning clear. *Les paroles*, whether applied to several people or to several semiotic systems, has been translated by various periphrases which we hope do not obscure the identity of meaning.

tially an individual act of selection and actualization; it is made in the first place of the 'combination thanks to which the speaking subject can use the code of the language with a view to expressing his personal thought' (this extended speech could be called *discourse*), and secondly by the 'psycho-physical mechanisms which allow him to exteriorize these combinations.' It is certain that phonation, for instance, cannot be confused with the language; neither the institution nor the system are altered if the individual who resorts to them speaks loudly or softly, with slow or rapid delivery, etc. The combinative aspect of speech is of course of capital importance, for it implies that speech is constituted by the recurrence of identical signs: it is because signs are repeated in successive discourses and within one and the same discourse (although they are combined in accordance with the infinite diversity of various people's speech) that each sign becomes an element of the language; and it is because speech is essentially a combinative activity that it corresponds to an individual act and not to a pure creation.

I.1.4. *The dialectics of language and speech:* Language and speech: each of these two terms of course achieves its full definition only in the dialectical process which unites one to the other: there is no language without speech, and no speech outside language: it is in this exchange that the real linguistic *praxis* is situated, as Merleau-Ponty has pointed out. And V. Brøndal writes, 'A language is a purely abstract entity, a norm which stands above individuals, a set of essential types, which speech actualizes in an infinite variety of ways.'[6] Language and speech are therefore in a relation of reciprocal comprehensiveness. On the one hand, the language is 'the treasure deposited by the practice of speech, in the subjects belonging to the same community' and, since it is a collective summa of individual imprints, it must remain incomplete at the level of each isolated individual: a language does not exist perfectly except in the 'speaking mass'; one cannot handle speech except by drawing on the language. But conversely, a language is possible only starting from speech: historically, speech phenomena always precede language phenomena (it is speech which makes language evolve), and genetically, a language is constituted in the individual through his learning from the environmental speech (one does not teach grammar and vocabulary which are, broadly speaking, the language, to babies). To sum, a language is at the same time the product and the instrument of speech: their relationship is therefore a genuinely dialectical one. It will be noticed (an important fact when we come to semiological prospects) that there could not possibly be (at least according to Saussure) a linguistics of speech, since any speech, as soon as it is grasped as a process of communication, is *already* part of the language: the latter only can be the object of a science. This disposes of two questions at the outset: it is useless to wonder whether speech must be studied *before* the language: the opposite is impossible: one can only study speech straight away inasmuch as it reflects the language (inasmuch as it is 'glottic'). It is just as useless to wonder *at the outset* how to separate the language from speech: this is no preliminary operation, but on the contrary the very essence of linguistic and later semiological investigation: to separate the language from speech means *ipso facto* constituting the problematics of the meaning.

I.1.5. *In Hjelmslev:* Hjelmslev[7] has not thrown over Saussure's conception of *language/speech*, but he has redistributed its terms in a more formal way. Within the language itself (which is still opposed to the act of speech) Hjelmslev distinguishes three planes: i) the *schema*, which is the language as pure form (before choosing this term Hjelmslev hesitated between 'system', 'pattern' or 'framework' for this plane):* this is Saussure's *langue* in the strictest sense of the word. It might mean, for instance, the French *r* as defined phonologically by its place in a series of oppositions; ii) the *norm*, which is the language as material form, after it has been defined by some degree of social realization, but still independent of this realization; it would mean the *r* in oral French, whichever way it is pronounced (but not that of written French); iii) the *usage*, which is the language as a set of habits prevailing in a given society: this would mean the *r* as it is pronounced in some regions. The relations of determination between speech, usage, norm and schema are varied: the norm determines usage and speech; usage determines speech

* Hjelmslev himself has suggested English, German and Danish translations for the terms he used in this article, which was written in French and published in the *Cahiers Ferdinand de Saussure*, 2, pp. 24–44 (1943). See *Essais Linguistiques*, p. 81, note 1. *Charpente* was a French alternative for *schéma*, 'pattern' was the English term suggested. But, following Hjelmslev's example when he rejected *système* in order not to give a too specific rendering (ibid., p. 72, note 1), we have preferred here to keep *schema* instead of the very general term 'pattern'. – Translators' note.

but is also determined by it; the schema is determined at the same time by speech, usage and norm. Thus appear (in fact) two fundamental planes: i) the *schema*, the theory of which merges with that of the form[8] and of the linguistic institution; ii) the group *norm-usage-speech*, the theory of which merges with that of the substance[9] and of the execution. As — according to Hjelmslev — norm is a pure methodical abstraction and speech a single concretion ('a transient document'), we find in the end a new dichotomy *schema/usage*, which replaces the couple *language/speech*. This redistribution by Hjelmslev is not without interest, however: it is a radical formalization of the concept of the language (under the name of *schema*) and eliminates concrete speech in favour of a more social concept: *usage*. This formalization of the language and socialization of speech enables us to put all the 'positive' and 'substantial' elements under the heading of speech, and all the differentiating ones under that of the language, and the advantage of this, as we shall see presently, is to remove one of the contradictions brought about by Saussure's distinction between the language and the speech.

I.1.6. *Some problems:* Whatever its usefulness and its fecundity, this distinction nevertheless brings some problems in its wake. Let us mention only three.

Here is the first: is it possible to identify the language with the code and the speech with the message? This identification is impossible according to Hjelmslev's theory. P. Guiraud refuses it for, he says, the conventions of the code are explicit, and those of the language implicit;[10] but it is certainly acceptable in the Saussurean framework, and A. Martinet takes it up.[11]

We encounter an analogous problem if we reflect on the relations between speech and syntagm.[12] Speech, as we have seen, can be defined (outside the variations of intensity in the phonation) as a (varied) combination of (recurrent) signs; but at the level of the language itself, however, there already exist some fixed syntagms (Saussure cites a compound word like *magnanimus*). The threshold which separates the language from speech may therefore be precarious, since it is here constituted by 'a certain degree of combination'. This leads to the question of an analysis of those fixed syntagms whose nature is nevertheless linguistic (glottic) since they are treated as one by paradigmatic variation (Hjelmslev calls this analysis morpho-syntax). Saussure had noticed this phenomenon of transition : 'there is probably also a whole series of sentences which belong to the language, and which the individual no longer has to combine himself.'[13] If these stereotypes belong to the language and no longer to speech, and if it proves true that numerous semiological systems use them to a great extent, then it is a real *linguistics of the syntagm* that we must expect, which will be used for all strongly stereotyped 'modes of writing'.

Finally, the third problem we shall indicate concerns the relations of the language with relevance (that is to say, with the signifying element proper in the unit). The language and relevance have sometimes been identified (by Trubetzkoy himself), thus thrusting outside the language all the non-relevant elements, that is, the combinative variants. Yet this identification raises a problem, for there are combinative variants (which therefore at first sight are a speech phenomenon) which are nevertheless *imposed*, that is to say, arbitrary : in French, it is required by the language that the *l* should be voiceless after a voiceless consonant (*oncle*) and voiced after a voiced consonant (*ongle*) without these facts leaving the realm of phonetics to belong to that of phonology. We see the theoretical consequences : must we admit that, contrary to Saussure's affirmation ('in the language there are only differences'), elements which are not differentiating can all the same belong to the language (to the institution)? Martinet thinks so; Frei attempts to extricate Saussure from the contradiction by localizing the differences in *subphonemes*, so that, for instance, *p* could not be differentiating in itself, but only, in it, the consonantic, occlusive voiceless labial features, etc. We shall not here take sides on this question; from a semiological point of view, we shall only remember the necessity of accepting the existence of syntagms and variations which are not signifying and are yet 'glottic', that is, belonging to the language. This linguistics, hardly foreseen by Saussure, can assume a great importance wherever fixed syntagms (or stereotypes) are found in abundance, which is probably the case in mass-languages, and every time non-signifying variations form a second-order corpus of signifiers, which is the case in strongly connated languages : [14] the rolled *r* is a mere combinative variant at the denotative level, but in the speech of the theatre, for instance, it signals a country accent and therefore is a part of a code, without which the message of 'ruralness' could not be either emitted or perceived.

I.1.7. *The idiolect:* To finish on the subject of *language/speech* in linguistics, we shall indicate two appended concepts isolated since Saussure's day. The first is that of the *idiolect*.[15] This is 'the language inasmuch as it is spoken by a single individual' (Martinet), or again 'the whole set of habits of a single individual at a given moment' (Ebeling). Jakobson has questioned the interest of this notion: the language is always socialized, even at the individual level, for in speaking to somebody one always tries to speak more or less the other's language, especially as far as the vocabulary is concerned ('private property in the sphere of language does not exist'): so the idiolect would appear to be largely an illusion. We shall nevertheless retain from this notion the idea that it can be useful to designate the following realities: i) the language of the aphasic who does not understand other people and does not receive a message conforming to his own verbal patterns; this language, then, would be a pure idiolect (Jakobson); ii) the 'style' of a writer, although this is always pervaded by certain verbal patterns coming from tradition that is, from the community; iii) finally, we can openly broaden the notion, and define the idiolect as the language of a linguistic community, that is, of a group of persons who all interpret in the same way all linguistic statements: the idiolect would then correspond roughly to what we have attempted to describe elsewhere under the name of 'writing'.[16] We can say in general that the hesitations in defining the concept of idiolect only reflect the need for an intermediate entity between speech and language (as was already proved by the *usage* theory in Hjelmslev), or, if you like, the need for a speech which is already institutionalized but not yet radically open to formalization, as the language is.

I.1.8. *Duplex Structures:* If we agree to identify *language/speech* and *code/message*, we must here mention a second appended concept which Jakobson has elaborated under the name of *duplex structures*; we shall do so only briefly, for his exposition of it has been reprinted.[17] We shall merely point out that under the name '*duplex structures*' Jakobson studies certain special cases of the general relation *code/ message* : two cases of circularity and two cases of overlapping. i) reported speech, or messages within a message (M/M): this is the general case of indirect styles. ii) proper names : the name signifies any person to whom this name is attributed and the circularity of the code is evident (C/C): *John means a person named John*; iii) cases of autonymy ('*Rat* is a syllable') : the word is here used as its own designation, the message overlaps the code (M/C) – this structure is important, for it covers the 'elucidating interpretations', namely, circumlocutions, synonyms and translations from one language into another; iv) the *shifters* are probably the most interesting double structure : the most ready example is that of the personal pronoun (*I, thou*) an indicial symbol which unites within itself the conventional and the existential bonds : for it is only by virtue of a conventional rule that *I* represents its object (so that *I* becomes *ego* in Latin, *ich* in German, etc.), but on the other hand, since it designates the person who utters it, it can only refer existentially to the utterance (C/M). Jakobson reminds us that personal pronouns have long been thought to be the most primitive layer of language

(Humboldt), but that in his view, they point rather to a complex and adult relationship between the code and the message: the personal pronouns are the last elements to be acquired in the child's speech and the first to be lost in aphasia; they are terms of transference which are difficult to handle. The *shifter* theory seems as yet to have been little exploited; yet it is, *a priori*, very fruitful to observe the code struggling with the message, so to speak (the converse being much more commonplace); perhaps (this is only a working hypothesis) it is on this side, that of the *shifters*, which are, as we saw, indicial symbols according to Peirce's terminology, that we should seek the semiological definition of the messages which stand on the frontiers of language, notably certain forms of literary discourse.

I.2. SEMIOLOGICAL PROSPECTS

I.2.1. *The language, speech and the social sciences.* The sociological scope of the *language/speech* concept is obvious. The manifest affinity of the language according to Saussure and of Durkheim's conception of a collective consciousness independent of its individual manifestations has been emphasized very early on. A direct influence of Durkheim on Saussure has even been postulated; it has been alleged that Saussure had followed very closely the debate between Durkheim and Tarde and that his conception of the language came from Durkheim while that of speech was a kind of concession to Tarde's idea on the individual element.[18] This hypothesis has lost some of its topicality because linguistics has chiefly developed, in the Saussurean idea of the language, the 'system of values' aspect, which led to acceptance of the necessity for an immanent analysis of the linguistic institution, and this immanence is inimical to sociological research.

Paradoxically, it is not therefore in the realm of sociology that the best development of the notion of *language/speech* will be found; it is in philosophy, with Merleau-Ponty, who was probably one of the first French philosophers to become interested in Saussure. He took up again the Saussurean distinction as an opposition between *speaking speech* (a signifying intention in its nascent state) and *spoken speech* (an 'acquired wealth' of the language which does recall Saussure's 'treasure').[19] He also broadened the notion by postulating that any *process* presupposes a *system*:[20] thus there has been elaborated an opposition between *event* and *structure* which has become accepted[21] and whose fruitfulness in history is well known.[22]

Saussure's notion has, of course, also been taken over and elaborated in the field of anthropology. The reference to Saussure is too explicit in the whole work of Claude Lévi-Strauss for us to need to insist on it; we shall simply remind the reader of three facts: i) That the opposition between process and system (speech and language) is found again in a concrete guise in the transition from the exchange of women to the structures of kinship; ii) that for Lévi-Strauss this opposition has an epistemological value: the study of linguistic phenomena is the domain of mechanistic (in Lévi-Strauss's sense of the word, namely, as opposed to 'statistical') and structural interpretation, and the study of speech phenomena is the domain of the theory of probabilities (macro-linguistics);[23] iii) finally, that the *unconscious* character of the language in those who draw on it for their speech, which is explicitly postulated by Saussure,[24] is again found in one of the most original and fruitful contentions of Lévi-Strauss, which states that it is not the contents which are unconscious (this is a criticism of Jung's archetypes) but the forms, that is, the symbolical function.

This idea is akin to that of Lacan, according to whom the libido itself is articulated as a system of significations, from which there follows, or will have to follow, a new type of description of the collective field of imagination, not by means of its 'themes', as has been done until now, but by its forms and its functions. Or let us say, more broadly but more clearly : by its signifiers more than by its signifieds.

It can be seen from these brief indications how rich in extra- or meta-linguistic developments the notion *language/speech* is. We shall therefore postulate that there exists a general category *language/speech*, which embraces all the systems of signs; since there are no better ones, we shall keep the terms *language* and *speech*, even when they are applied to communications whose substance is not verbal.

I.2.2. *The garment system:* We saw that the separation between the language and speech represented the essential feature of linguistic analysis; it would therefore be futile to propose to apply this separation straightaway to systems of objects, images or behaviour patterns which have not yet been studied from a semantic point of view. We can merely, in the case of some of these hypothetical systems, foresee that certain classes of facts will belong to the category of the *language* and others to that of *speech*, and make it immediately clear that in the course of its application to semiology, Saussure's distinction is likely to undergo modifications which it will be precisely our task to note.

Let us take the garment system for instance; it is probably necessary to subdivide it into three different systems, according to which substance is used for communication.

In clothes as *written* about, that is to say described in a fashion magazine by means of articulated language, there is practically no 'speech': the garment which is described never corresponds to an individual handling of the rules of fashion, it is a systematized set of signs and rules: it is a language in its pure state. According to the Saussurean schema, a language without speech would be impossible; what makes the fact acceptable here is, on the one hand, that the language of fashion does not emanate from the 'speaking mass' but from a group which makes the decisions and deliberately elaborates the code, and on the other hand that the abstraction inherent in any language is here materialized as written language: fashion clothes (as written about) are the language at the level of vestimentary communication and speech at the level of verbal communication.

In clothes as *photographed* (if we suppose, to simplify matters, that there is no duplication by verbal description), the language still issues from the fashion group, but it is no longer given in a wholly abstract form, for a photographed garment is always worn by an individual woman. What is given by the fashion photograph is a semi-formalized state of the garment system: for on the one hand, the language of fashion must here be inferred from a pseudo-real garment, and on the other, the wearer of the garment (the photographed model) is, so to speak, a normative individual, chosen for her canonic generality, and who consequently represents a 'speech' which is fixed and devoid of all combinative freedom.

Finally in clothes as *worn* (or real clothes), as Trubetzkoy had suggested,[25] we again find the classic distinction between language and speech. The language, in the garment system, is made i) by the oppositions of pieces, parts of garment and 'details', the variation of which entails a change in meaning (to wear a beret or a bowler hat does not have the same meaning); ii) by the rules which govern the association of the pieces among themselves, either on the length of the body or in depth. Speech, in the garment system, comprises all the phenomena of anomic fabrication (few are still left in our society) or of individual way of wearing (size of the garment, degree of cleanliness or wear, personal quirks, free association of pieces). As for the dialectic which unites here costume (the language) and clothing (speech), it does not resemble that of verbal language; true, clothing always draws on costume (except in the case of eccentricity, which, by the way, also has its signs), but costume, at least today, *precedes* clothing, since it comes from the ready-made industry, that is, from a minority group (although more anonymous than that of Haute Couture).

I.2.3. *The food system:* Let us now take another signifying system: food. We shall find there without difficulty Saussure's distinction. The alimentary language is made of i) rules of exclusion (alimentary taboos); ii) signifying oppositions of units, the type of which remains to be determined (for instance the type *savoury/sweet*); iii) rules of association, either simultaneous (at the level of a dish) or successive (at the level of a menu); iv) rituals of use which function, perhaps, as a kind of alimentary *rhetoric*. As for alimentary 'speech', which is very rich, it comprises all the personal (or family) variations of preparation and association (one might consider cookery within one family, which is subject to a number of habits, as an idiolect). The *menu*, for instance, illustrates very well this relationship between the language and speech: any menu is concocted with reference to a structure (which is both national – or regional – and social); but this structure is filled differently according to the days and the users, just as a linguistic 'form' is filled by the free variations and combinations which a speaker needs for a particular message. The relationship between the language and speech would here be fairly similar to that which is found in verbal language: broadly, it is usage, that is to say, a sort of sedimentation of many people's speech, which makes up the alimentary language; however, phenomena of individual innovation can acquire an institutional value within it. What is missing, in any case, contrary to what happened in the garment system, is the action of a deciding group: the alimentary language is evolved only from a broadly collective usage, or from a purely individual speech.

I.2.4. *The car system, the furniture system:* To bring to a close, somewhat arbitrarily, this question of the prospects opened up by the *language/speech* distinction, we shall mention a few more suggestions concerning two systems of objects, very different, it is true, but which have in common a dependence in each case on a deciding and manufacturing group : cars and furniture.

In the car system, the language is made up by a whole set of forms and details, the structure of which is established differentially by comparing the prototypes to each other (independently of the number of their 'copies'); the scope of 'speech' is very narrow because, for a given status of buyer, freedom in choosing a model is very restricted : it can involve only two or three models, and within each model, colour and fittings. But perhaps we should here exchange the notion of cars as *objects* for that of cars as sociological facts; we would then find in the *driving* of cars the variations in usage of the object which usually make up the plane of speech. For the user cannot in this instance have a direct action on the model and combine its units; his freedom of interpretation is found in the usage developed in time and within which the 'forms' issuing from the language must, in order to become actual, be relayed by certain practices.

Finally, the last system about which we should like to say a word, that of furniture, is also a semantic object : the 'language' is formed both by the oppositions of functionally identical pieces (two types of wardrobe, two types of bed, etc), each of which, according to its 'style', refers to a different meaning, and by the rules of association of the different units at the level of a room ('furnishing'); the 'speech' is here formed either by the insignificant variations which the user can introduce into one unit (by tinkering with one element, for instance), or by freedom in associating pieces of furniture together.

I.2.5. *Complex systems:* The most interesting systems, at least among those which belong to the province of mass-communications, are complex systems in which different substances are engaged. In cinema, television and advertising, the senses are subjected to the concerted action of a collection of images, sounds and written words. It will, therefore, be premature to decide, in their case, which facts belong to the language and which belong to speech, on the one hand as long as one has not discovered whether the 'language' of each of these complex systems is original or only compounded of the subsidiary 'languages' which have their places in them, and on the other hand as long as these subsidiary languages have not been analysed (we know the linguistic 'language', but not that of images or that of music).

As for the Press, which can be reasonably considered as an autonomous signifying system, even if we confine ourselves to its written elements only, we are still almost entirely ignorant of a linguistic phenomenon which seems to play an essential part in it: connotation, that is, the development of a system of second-order meanings, which are so to speak parasitic on the language proper.[26] This second-order system is also a 'language', within which there develop speech-phenomena, idiolects and duplex structures. In the case of such complex or connoted systems (both characteristics are not mutually exclusive), it is therefore no longer possible to predetermine, even in global and hypothetical fashion, what belongs to the language and what belongs to speech.

I.2.6. Problems (1) – the origin of the various signifyings systems: The semiological extension of the *language/speech* notion brings with it some problems, which of course coincide with the points where the linguistic model can no longer be followed and must be altered. The first problem concerns the origin of the various systems, and thus touches on the very dialectics of language and speech. In the linguistic model, nothing enters the language without having been tried in speech, but conversely no speech is possible (that is, fulfils its function of communication) if it is not drawn from the 'treasure' of the language. This process is still, at least partially, found in a system like that of food, although individual innovations brought into it can become language phenomena. But in most other semiological systems, the language is elaborated not by the 'speaking mass' but by a deciding group. In this sense, it can be held that in most semiological languages, the sign is really and truly 'arbitrary'[27] since it is founded in artificial fashion by a unilateral decision; these in fact are fabricated languages, 'logo-techniques'. The user follows these languages, draws messages (or 'speech') from them but has no part in their elaboration. The deciding group which is at the origin of the system (and of its changes) can be more or less narrow; it can be a highly qualified technocracy (fashion, motor industry); it can also be a more diffuse and anonymous group (the production of standardized furniture, the middle reaches of ready-to-wear). If, however, this artificial character does not alter the institutional nature of the communication and preserves some amount of dialectical play between the system and usage, it is because, in the first place, although imposed on the users, the signifying 'contract' is no less observed by the great majority of them (otherwise the user is *marked* with a certain 'asociability' : he can no longer communicate anything except his eccentricity); and because, moreover, languages elaborated as the outcome of a decision are not entirely free ('arbitrary'). They are subject to the determination of the community, at least through the following agencies : i) when new needs are born, following the development of societies (the move to semi-European clothing in contemporary African countries, the birth of new patterns of quick feeding in industrial and urban societies); ii) when economic requirements bring about the disappearance or promotion of certain materials (artificial textiles); iii) when ideology limits the invention of forms, subjects it to taboos and reduces, so to speak, the margins of the 'normal'. In a wider sense, we can say that the elaborations of deciding groups, namely the logo-techniques, are themselves only the terms of an ever-widening function, which is the collective field of imagination of the epoch : thus individual innovation is transcended by a sociological determination (from restricted groups), but these sociological determinations refer in turn to a final meaning, which is anthropological.

I.2.7. *Problems (II) – the proportion between 'language' and 'speech' in the various systems:* The second problem presented by the semiological extension of the *language/speech* notion is centred on the proportion, in the matter of volume, which can be established between the 'language' and the corresponding 'speech' in any system. In verbal language there is a very great disproportion between the language, which is a finite set of rules, and speech, which comes under the heading of these rules and is practically unlimited in its variety. It can be presumed that the food system still offers an important difference in the volume of each, since within the culinary 'forms', the modalities and combinations in interpretation are numerous. But we have seen that in the car or the furniture system the scope for combinative variations and free associations is small : there is very little margin – at least of the sort which is acknowledged by the institution itself – between the model and its 'execution' : these are systems in which 'speech' is poor. In a particular system, that of written fashion, speech is even almost non-existent, so that we are dealing here, paradoxically, with a language without speech (which is possible, as we have seen, only because this language is upheld by linguistic speech).

The fact remains that if it is true that there are languages without speech or with a very restricted speech, we shall have to revise the Saussurean theory which states that a language is nothing but a system of differences (in which case, being entirely negative, it cannot be grasped outside speech). and complete the couple *language/speech* with a third, presignifying element, a matter or substance providing the (necessary) support of signification. In a phrase like *a long or short dress*, the 'dress' is only the support of a variant (*long/short*) which *does* fully belong to the garment language – a distinction which is unknown in ordinary language, in which, since the sound is considered as *immediately* significant, it cannot be decomposed into an inert and a semantic element. This would lead us to recognize in (nonlinguistic) semiological systems three (and not two) planes: that of the matter, that of the language and that of the usage. This of course allows us to account for systems without 'execution', since the first element ensures that there is a materiality of the language; and such a modification is all the more plausible since it can be explained genetically: if, in such systems, the 'language' needs a 'matter' (and no longer a 'speech'), it is because unlike that of human language their origin is in general utilitarian, and not signifying.

II. SIGNIFIER AND SIGNIFIED

II.1. THE SIGN

II.1.1. *The classification of signs:* The signified and the signifier, in Saussurean terminology, are the components of the *sign*. Now this term, *sign*, which is found in very different vocabularies (from that of theology to that of medicine), and whose history is very rich (running from the Gospels[28] to cybernetics), is for these very reasons very ambiguous; so before we come back to the Saussurean acceptance of the word, we must say a word about the notional field in which it occupies a place, albeit imprecise, as will be seen. For, according to the arbitrary choice of various authors, the sign is placed in a series of terms which have affinities and dissimilarities with it : *signal, index, icon, symbol, allegory*, are the chief rivals of *sign*. Let us first state the element which is common to all these terms : they all necessarily refer us to a *relation* between two *relata*.[29] This feature cannot therefore be used to distinguish any of the terms in the series; to find a variation in meaning, we shall have to resort to other features, which will be expressed here in the form of an alternative (*presence/absence*): i) the relation implies, or does not imply, the mental representation of one of the *relata*; ii) the relation implies, or does not imply, an analogy between the *relata*; iii) the link between the two *relata* (the stimulus and its response) is immediate or is not; iv) the *relata* exactly coincide or, on the contrary, one overruns the other; v) the relation implies, or does not imply, an existential connection with the user.[30] Whether these features are positive or negative (marked or unmarked), each term in the field is differentiated from its neighbours. It must be added that the distribution of the field varies from one author to another, a fact which produces terminological contradictions; these will be easily seen at a glance from a table of the incidence of features and terms in four different authors: Hegel, Peirce, Jung and Wallon (the reference to some features, whether marked or unmarked, may be absent in some authors). We see that the terminological contradiction bears essentially on *index* (for Peirce, the index is existential, for Wallon, it is not) and on *symbol* (for Hegel and Wallon there is a relation of analogy – or of 'motivation' – between the two *relata of* the symbol, but not for Peirce; moreover, for Peirce, the symbol is not existential, whereas it is for Jung). But we see also that these contradictions – which in this table are read vertically – are very well explained, or rather, that they compensate each other through transfers of meaning from term to term in the same author. These transfers can here be read horizontally : for instance, the symbol is analogical in Hegel as opposed to the sign which is not; and if it is not in Peirce, it is because the icon can absorb that feature. All this means, to sum up and talk in semiological terms (this being the point of this brief analysis which reflects, like a mirror, the subject and methods of our study), that the words in the field derive their

	signal	index	icon	symbol	sign	allegory
1. Mental representation	Wallon −	Wallon −		Wallon +	Wallon +	
2. Analogy			Peirce +	Hegel + Wallon + Peirce −	Hegel − Wallon −	
3. Immediacy	Wallon +	Wallon −				
4. Adequacy	Wallon +			Hegel − Jung − Wallon −	Hegel + Jung + Wallon +	
5. Existential aspect	Wallon +	Wallon − Peirce +		Peirce − Jung +		Jung −

meaning only from their opposition to one another (usually in pairs), and that if these oppositions are preserved, the meaning is unambiguous. In particular, *signal* and *index*, *symbol* and *sign*, are the terms of two different functions, which can themselves be opposed as a whole, as they do in Wallon, whose terminology is the clearest and the most complete[31] (*icon* and *allegory* are confined to the vocabulary of Peirce and Jung). We shall therefore say, with Wallon, that the *signal* and the *index* form a group of *relata* devoid of mental representation, whereas in the opposite group, that of *symbol* and *sign*, this representation exists; furthermore, the *signal* is immediate and existential, whereas the *index* is not (it is only a trace); finally, that in the *symbol* the representation is analogical and inadequate (Christianity 'outruns' the cross), whereas in the *sign* the relation is un-motivated and exact (there is no analogy between the word *ox* and the image of an *ox*, which is per-fectly covered by its *relatum*).

II.1.2. *The linguistic sign:* In linguistics, the notion of sign does not give rise to any competition between neighbouring terms. When he sought to designate the signifying relationship, Saussure immediately eliminated *symbol* (because the term implied the idea of motivation) in favour of *sign* which he defined as the union of a signifier and a signified (in the fashion of the recto and verso of a sheet of paper), or else of an acoustic image and a concept. Until he found the words *signifier* and *signified*, however, *sign* remained ambiguous, for it tended to become identified with the signifier only, which Saussure wanted at all costs to avoid; after having hesitated between *sôme* and *sème*, *form* and *idea*, *image* and *concept*, Saussure settled upon *signifier* and *signified*, the union of which forms the sign. This is a paramount proposition, which one must always bear in mind, for there is a tendency to interpret *sign* as signifier, whereas this is a two-sided Janus-like entity. The (important) consequence is that, for Saussure, Hjelmslev and Frei at least, since the signifieds are signs among others, semantics must be a part of structural linguistics, whereas for the American mechanists the signifieds are substances which must be expelled from linguistics and left to psychology. Since Saussure, the theory of the linguistic sign has been enriched by the *double articulation* principle, the importance of which has been shown by Martinet, to the extent that he made it the criterion which defines language. For among linguistic signs, we must distinguish between the *significant units*, each one of which is endowed with one meaning (the 'words', or to be exact, the 'monemes') and which form the first articulation, and the *distinctive units*, which are part of the form but do not have a direct meaning ('the sounds', or rather the phonemes), and which constitute the second articulation. It is this double articulation which accounts for the economy of human language; for it is a powerful gearing-down which allows, for instance, American Spanish to produce, with only 21 distinctive units, 100,000 significant units.

II.1.3. *Form and substance:* The sign is therefore a compound of a signifier and a signified. The plane of the signifiers constitutes the *plane of expression* and that of the signifieds the *plane of content*. Within each of these two planes, Hjelmslev has introduced a distinction which may be important for the study of the semiological (and no longer only linguistic) sign. According to him, each plane comprises two *strata* : *form* and *substance*; we must insist on the new definition of these two terms, for each of them has a weighty lexical past. The *form* is what can be described exhaustively, simply and coherently (epistemological criteria) by linguistics without resorting to any extralinguistic premise; the *substance* is the whole set of aspects of linguistic phenomena which cannot be described without resorting to extralinguistic premises. Since both *strata* exist on the plane of expression and the plane of content, we therefore have : i) a substance of expression : for instance the phonic, articulatory, non-functional substance which is the field of phonetics, not phonology; ii) a form of expression, made of the paradigmatic and syntactic rules (let us note that the same form can have two different substances, one phonic, the other graphic); iii) a substance of content : this includes, for instance, the emotional, ideological, or simply notional aspects of the signified, its 'positive' meaning; iv) a form of content : it is the formal organization of the signified among themselves through the absence or presence of a semantic mark.[32] This last notion is difficult to grasp, because of the impossibility of separating the signifiers from the signifieds in human language; but for this very reason the subdivision *form/substance* can be made more useful and easier to handle in semiology, in the following cases : i) when we deal with a system in which the signifieds are substantified in a substance other than that of their own system (this is, as we have seen, the case with fashion as it is written about); ii) when a system of objects includes a substance which is not immediately and functionally significant, but can be, at a certain level, simply utilitarian : the function of a dish can be to signify a situation and also to serve as food.

II.1.4. *The semiological sign:* This perhaps allows us to foresee the nature of the semiological sign in relation to the linguistic sign. The semiological sign is also, like its model, compounded of a signifier and a signified (the colour of a light, for instance, is an order to move on, in the Highway Code), but it differs from it at the level of its substances. Many semiological systems (objects, gestures, pictorial images)[33] have a substance of expression whose essence is not to signify; often, they are objects of everyday use, used by society in a derivative way, to signify something: clothes are used for protection and food for nourishment even if they are also used as signs. We propose to call these semiological signs, whose origin is utilitarian and functional, *sign-functions.* The sign-function bears witness to a double movement, which must be taken apart. In a first stage (this analysis is purely operative and does not imply real temporality) the function becomes pervaded with meaning. This semantization is inevitable : *as soon as there is a society, every usage is converted into a sign of itself;* the use of a raincoat is to give protection from the rain, but this use cannot be dissociated from the very signs of an atmospheric situation. Since our society produces only standardized, normalized objects, these objects are unavoidably realizations of a model, the speech of a language, the substances of a significant form. To rediscover a non-signifying object, one

would have to imagine a utensil absolutely impro-
vised and with no similarity to an existing model
(Lévi-Strauss has shown to what extent tinkering
about is itself the search for a meaning): a hypothesis
which is virtually impossible to verify in any society.
This universal semantization of the usages is crucial:
it expresses the fact that there is no reality except
when it is intelligible, and should eventually lead to
the merging of sociology with socio-logic.[34] But once
the sign is constituted, society can very well re-
functionalize it, and speak about it as if it were an
object made for use: a fur-coat will be described as
if it served only to protect from the cold. This recurrent functionalization, which needs, in order to
exist, a second-order language, is by no means the
same as the first (and indeed purely ideal) functionalization: for the function which is re-presented does
in fact correspond to a second (disguised) semantic
institutionalization, which is of the order of connotation. The sign-function therefore has (probably) an
anthropological value, since it is the very unit where
the relations of the technical and the significant are
woven together.

II.2. THE SIGNIFIED

II.2.1. *Nature of the signified:* In linguistics, the
nature of the signified has given rise to discussions
which have centred chiefly on its degree of 'reality';
all agree, however, on emphasizing the fact that the
signified is not 'a thing' but a mental representation
of the 'thing'. We have seen that in the definition of
the sign by Wallon, this representative character was

a relevant feature of the sign and the symbol (as opposed to the index and the signal). Saussure himself has clearly marked the mental nature of the signified by calling it a *concept*: the signified of the word *ox* is not the animal *ox*, but its mental image (this will prove important in the subsequent discussion on the nature of the sign).[35] These discussions, however, still bear the stamp of psychologism, so the analysis of the Stoics[36] will perhaps be thought preferable. They carefully distinguished the ϛαντασία λογική (the mental representation), the τυγχανόν (the real thing) and the λεκτόν (the utterable). The signified is neither the φαντασία nor the τυγχανόν, but rather the λεκτυν; being neither an act of consciousness, nor a real thing, it can be defined only within the signifying process, in a quasi-tautological way: it is this 'something' which is meant by the person who uses the sign. In this way we are back again to a purely functional definition: the signified is one of the two *relata* of the sign; the only difference which opposes it to the signified is that the latter is a mediator. The situation could not be essentially different in semiology, where objects, images, gestures, etc., inasmuch as they are significant, refer back to something which can be expressed only through them, except that the semiological signified can be taken up by the linguisitic signs. One can say, for instance, that a certain sweater means *long autumn walks in the woods*; in this case, the signified is mediated not only by its vestimentary signifier (the sweater), but also by a fragment of speech (which greatly helps in handling it). We could give the name of *isology* to the phenomenon whereby language wields its signifiers and signifieds so that it is impossible to dissociate and differentiate them, in order to set aside the case of the non-isologic systems (which are inevitably complex), in which the signified can be simply *juxtaposed* with its signifier.

II.2.2. *Classification of the linguistic signifieds:* How can we classify the signifieds? We know that in semiology this operation is fundamental, since it amounts to isolating the *form* from the content. As far as linguistic signifiers are concerned, two sorts of classification can be conceived. The first is external, and makes use of the 'positive' (and not purely differential) content of concepts: this is the case in the methodical groupings of Hallig and Wartburg,[37] and in the more convincing notional fields of Trier and lexicological fields of Matoré.[38] But from a structural point of view, this classification (especially those of Hallig and Wartburg) have the defect of resting still too much on the (ideological) *substance* of the signifieds, and not on their *form*. To succeed in establishing a really formal classification, one would have to succeed in reconstituting oppositions of signifieds, and in isolating, within each one of these, a relevant commutative feature:[39] this method has been advocated by Hjelmslev, Sörensen, Prieto and Greimas. Hjelmslev, for instance, decomposes a moneme like 'mare' into two smaller significant units: 'Horse' + 'female', and these units can be commutated and therefore used to reconstitute new monemes ('pig' + 'female' = 'sow', 'horse' + 'male' = 'stallion'); Prieto sees in 'vir' two commutable features 'homo' + 'masculus'; Sörensen reduces the lexicon of kinship to a combination of 'primitives' ('father' = male parent, 'parent' = first ascendent). None of these analyses has yet been developed.[40] Finally, we must remind the reader that according to some linguists, the signifieds are not a part of linguistics, which is concerned only with signifiers, and that semantic classification lies outside the field of linguistics.[41]

II.2.3. *The semiological signifieds:* Structural linguistics, however advanced, has not yet elaborated a semantics, that is to say a classification of the *forms* of the verbal signified. One may therefore easily imagine that it is at present impossible to put forward a classification of semiological signifieds, unless we choose to fall back on to known notional fields. We shall venture three observations only.

The first concerns the mode of actualization of semiological signifieds. These can occur either isologically or not; in the latter case, they are taken up, through articulated language, either by a word (*week-end*) or by a group of words (*long walks in the country*); they are thereby easier to handle, since the analyst is not forced to impose on them his own metalanguage, but also more dangerous, since they ceaselessly refer back to the semantic classification of the language itself (which is itself unknown), and not to a classification having its bases in the system under observation. The signifieds of the fashion garment, even if they are mediated by the speech of the magazine, are not necessarily distributed like the signifieds of the language, since they do not always have the same 'length' (here a word, there a sentence). In the first case, that of the isologic systems, the signified has no materialization other than its typical signifier; one cannot therefore handle it except by imposing on it a metalanguage. One can for instance ask some subjects about the meaning they attribute to a piece of music by submitting to them a list of verbalized signifieds (*anguished, stormy, sombre, tormented*, etc.);[42] whereas in fact all these verbal signs for a single musical signified, which ought to be designated by one single cipher, which would imply no verbal dissection and no metaphorical small change. These metalanguages, issuing from the analyst in the former case, and the system itself in the latter, are probably inevitable, and this is what still makes the analysis of the signifieds, or ideological analysis, problematical; its place within the semiological project will at least have to be defined in theory.

Our second remark concerns the extension of the semiological signifieds. The whole of the signifieds of a system (once formalized) constitutes a great function; now it is probable that from one system to the other, the great semiological functions not only communicate, but also partly overlap; the form of the signified in the garment system is probably partly the same as that of the signified in the food system, being, as they are, both articulated on the large-scale opposition of work and festivity, activity and leisure. One must therefore foresee a total ideological description, common to all the systems of a given synchrony.

Finally – and this will be our third remark – we may consider that to each system of signifiers (lexicons) there corresponds, on the plane of the signifieds, a corpus of practices and techniques; these collections of signifieds imply on the part of system consumers (of 'readers', that is to say), different degrees of knowledge (according to differences in their 'culture'), which explains how the same 'lexie' (or large unit of reading) can be deciphered differently according to the individuals concerned, without ceasing to belong to a given 'language'. Several lexicons – and consequently several bodies of signifieds – can coexist within the same individual, determining in each one more or less 'deep' readings.

II.3. THE SIGNIFIER

II.3.1. *Nature of the signifier:* The nature of the signifier suggests roughly the same remarks as that of the signified: it is purely a *relatum*, whose definition cannot be separated from that of the signified. The only difference is that the signifier is a mediator: some matter is necessary to it. But on the one hand it is not sufficient to it, and on the other, in semiology, the signifier can, too, be relayed by a certain matter: that of words. This materiality of the signifier makes it once more necessary to distinguish clearly *matter* from *substance*: a substance can be immaterial (in the case of the substance of the content); therefore, all one can say is that the substance of the signifier is always material (sounds, objects, images). In semiology, where we shall have to deal with mixed systems in which different kinds of matter are involved (sound and image, object and writing, etc.), it may be appropriate to collect together all the signs, *inasmuch as they are borne by one and the same matter*, under the concept of the *typical sign*: the verbal sign, the graphic sign, the iconic sign, the gestural sign are all typical signs.

II.3.2. *Classification of the signifiers:* The classification of the signifiers is nothing but the structuraliza-
tion proper of the system. What has to be done is to
cut up the 'endless' message constituted by the whole
of the messages emitted at the level of the studied
corpus, into minimal significant units by means of
the commutation test,[43] then to group these units
into paradigmatic classes, and finally to classify the
syntagmatic relations which link these units. These
operations constitute an important part of the semiological undertaking which will be dealt with in chapter
III; we anticipate the point in mentioning it here.[44]

II.4. THE SIGNIFICATION

II.4.1. *The significant correlation:* The sign is a (two-
faced) slice of sonority, visuality, etc. The *signification* can be conceived as a process; it is the act which
binds the signifier and the signified, an act whose product is the sign. This distinction has, of course, only
a classifying (and not phenomenological) value:
firstly, because the union of signifier and signified, as
we shall see, does not exhaust the semantic act, for
the sign derives its value also from its surroundings;
secondly, because, probably, the mind does not pro-
ceed, in the semantic process, by conjunction but by
carving out.[45] And indeed the signification (*semiosis*)
does not unite unilateral entities, it does not conjoin
two terms, for the very good reason that signifier and
signified are both at once term and relation.[46] This
ambiguity makes any graphic representation of the
signification somewhat clumsy, yet this operation is

necessary for any semiological discourse. On this point, let us mention the following attempts:

1) $\frac{Sr}{Sd}$: In Saussure, the sign appears, in his demonstration, as the vertical extension of a situation *in depth*: in the language, the signified is, as it were, *behind* the signifier, and can be reached only through it, although, on the one hand, these excessively spatial metaphors miss the dialectical nature of the signification, and on the other hand the 'closed' character of the sign is acceptable only for the frankly discontinuous systems, such as that of the language.

2) ERC: Hjelmslev has chosen in preference a purely graphic representation: there is a relation (R) between the plane of expression (E) and the plane of content (C). This formula enables us to account economically and without metaphorical falsification, for the metalanguages or derivative systems E R (ERC).[47]

3) $\frac{S}{s}$: Lacan, followed by Laplanche and Leclaire,[48] uses a spatialized writing which, however, differs from Saussure's representation on two points: i) the signifier (S) is global, made up of a multilevelled chain (metaphorical chain): signifier and signified have only a floating relationship and coincide only at certain anchorage points; ii) the line between the signifier (S) and the signified (s) has its own value (which of course it had not in Saussure): it represents the repression of the signified.

4) Sr ≡ Sd: Finally, in non-isologic systems (that is, those in which the signifieds are materialized through another system), it is of course legitimate to extend

49

the relation in the form of an equivalence ($\equiv$) but not of an identity ($=$).

II.4.2. *The arbitrary and the motivated in linguistics*: We have seen that all that could be said about the signifier is that it was a (material) mediator of the signified. What is the nature of this mediation? In linguistics, this problem has provoked some discussion, chiefly about terminology, for all is fairly clear about the main issues (this will perhaps not be the case with semiology). Starting from the fact that in human language the choice of sounds is not imposed on us by the meaning itself (the *ox* does not determine the sound *ox*, since in any case the sound is different in other languages), Saussure had spoken of an *arbitrary* relation between signifier and signified. Benveniste has questioned the aptness of this word:[49] what is arbitrary is the relation between the signifier and the 'thing' which is signified (of the sound *ox* and the animal the *ox*). But, as we have seen, even for Saussure, the sign is not the 'thing', but the mental representation of the thing (*concept*); the association of sound and representation is the outcome of a collective training (for instance the learning of the French tongue); this association – which is the signification – is by no means arbitrary (for no French person is free to modify it), indeed it is, on the contrary, necessary. It was therefore suggested to say that in linguistics the signification is *unmotivated*. This lack of motivation, is, by the way, only partial (Saussure speaks of a relative analogy): from signified to signifier, there is a certain motivation in the (restricted) case of onomatopoeia, as we shall see shortly, and also every time a series of signs is created by the tongue through the imitation of a certain prototype of composition or derivation: this is the case with so-called proportional signs: *pommier, poirer, abricotier*, etc., once the lack of motivation in their roots and their suffix is established, show an analogy in their composition. We shall therefore say in general terms that in the language the link between signifier and signified is contractual in its principle, but that this contract is collective, inscribed in a long temporality (Saussure says that 'a language is always a legacy'), and that consequently it is, as it were, *naturalized*; in the same way, Levi-Strauss specified that the linguistic sign is arbitrary *a priori* but non-arbitrary *a posteriori*. This discussion leads us to keep two different terms, which will be useful during the semiological extension. We shall say that a system is arbitrary when its signs are founded not by convention, but by unilateral decision: the sign is not arbitrary in the language but it is in fashion; and we shall say that a sign is *motivated* when the relation between its signified and its signifier is analogical (Buyssens has put forward, as suitable terms, *intrinsic semes* for motivated signs, and *extrinsic semes* for unmotivated ones). It will therefore be possible to have systems which are arbitrary and motivated, and others which are non-arbitrary and unmotivated.

II.4.3. *The arbitrary and the motivated in semiology:* In linguistics, motivation is limited to the partial plane of derivation or composition; in semiology, on the contrary, it will put to us more general problems. On the one hand, it is possible that outside language systems may be found, in which motivation plays a great part. We shall then have to establish in what way analogy is compatible with the discontinuous character which up to now has seemed necessary to signification; and afterwards how paradigmatic series (that is, in which the terms are few and discrete) can be established when the signifiers are *analoga*: this will probably be the case of 'images', the semiology of which is, for these reasons, far from being established. On the other hand, it is highly probable that a semiological inventory will reveal the existence of impure systems, comprising either very loose motivations, or motivations pervaded, so to speak, with secondary non-motivations, as if, often, the sign lent itself to a kind of conflict between the motivated and the unmotivated. This is already to some extent the case of the most 'motivated' zone of language, that of onomatopoeia. Martinet has pointed out[50] that the onomatopoeic motivation was accompanied by a loss of the double articulation (*ouch*, which depends only on the second articulation, replaces the doubly articulated syntagm '*it hurts*'); yet the onomatopoeia which expresses pain is not exactly the same in French (*aïe*) and in Danish (*au*), for instance. This is because in fact motivation here submits, as it were, to phonological models which of course vary with different languages: there is an impregnation of the analogical by the digital. Outside language, problematic systems, like the 'language' of the bees, show the same ambiguity: the honey-gathering dances have a vaguely analogical value; that at the entrance of the hive is frankly motivated (by the direction of the food), but the wriggly dance in a figure of eight is quite unmotivated (it refers to a distance).[51] Finally, and as a last example of such ill-defined areas,[52] certain trade-marks used in advertising consist of purely 'abstract' (non-analogical) shapes; they can, however, 'express' a certain impression (for instance one of 'power') which has a relation of affinity with the signified. The trade-mark of the Berliet lorries (a circle with a thick arrow across it) does not in any way 'copy' power – indeed, how could one 'copy' power? – and yet suggests it through a latent analogy; the same ambiguity is to be found in the signs of some ideographic writings (Chinese, for instance).

The coexistence of the analogical and the non-analogical therefore seems unquestionable, even within a single system. Yet semiology cannot be content with a description acknowledging this compromise without trying to systematize it, for it cannot admit a continuous differential since, as we shall see, meaning is articulation. These problems have not yet been studied in detail, and it would be impossible to give a general survey of them. The outline of an economy of signification (at the anthropological level) can, however, be perceived: in the language, for instance, the (relative) motivation introduces a certain order at the level of the first (significant) articulation: the 'contract' is therefore in this case underpinned by a certain naturalization of this *a priori* arbitrariness which Lévi-Strauss talks about; other systems, on the contrary, can go from motivation to non-motivation: for instance the set of the ritual puppets of initiation of the Senoufo, cited by Lévi-Strauss in *The Savage Mind*. It is therefore probable that at the level of the most general semiology, which merges with anthropology, there comes into being a sort of circularity between the analogical and the unmotivated: there is a double tendency (each aspect being complementary to the other) to naturalize the unmotivated and to intellectualize the motivated (that is to say, to culturalize it). Finally, some authors are confident that digitalism, which is the rival of the analogical, is itself in its purest form – binarism – a 'reproduction' of certain physiological processes, if it is true that sight and hearing, in the last analysis, function by alternative selections.[53]

II.5. VALUE

II.5.1. *Value in linguistics:* We have said, or at least hinted, that to treat the sign 'in itself', as the only link between signifier and signified, is a fairly arbitrary (although inevitable) abstraction. We must, to conclude, tackle the sign, no longer by way of its 'composition', but of its 'setting': this is the problem of value. Saussure did not see the importance of this notion at the outset, but even as early as his second *Course in General Linguistics*, he increasingly concentrated on it, and value became an essential concept for him, and eventually more important than that of signification (with which it is not co-extensive). Value bears a close relation to the notion of the language (as opposed to speech); its effect is to depsychologize linguistics and to bring it closer to economics; it is therefore central to structural linguistics. In most sciences, Saussure observes,[54] there is no coexistence of synchrony and diachrony: astronomy is a synchronic science (although the heavenly bodies alter); geology is a diachronic science (although it can study fixed states); history is mainly diachronic (a succession of events), although it can linger over some 'pictures'.[55] Yet there is a science in which these two aspects have an equal share: economics (which include economics proper, and economic history); the same applies to linguistics, Saussure goes on to say. This is because in both cases we are dealing with a system of equivalence between two different things: work and reward, a signifier and a signified (this is the phenomenon which we have up to now called *signification*). Yet, in linguistics as well as in economics, this equivalence is not isolated, for if we alter one of its terms, the whole system changes by degrees. For a sign (or an economic 'value') to exist, it must therefore be possible, on the one hand, to *exchange* dissimilar things (work and wage, signifier and signified), and on the other, to *compare* similar things with each other. One can exchange a five-franc note for bread, soap or a cinema ticket, but one can also compare this banknote with ten- or fifty-franc notes, etc.; in the same way, a 'word' can be 'exchanged' for an idea (that is, for something dissimilar), but it can also be compared with other words (that is, something similar): in English the word *mutton* derives its value only from its coexistence with *sheep*; the meaning is truly fixed only at the end of this double determination: signification and value. Value, therefore, is not signification; it comes, Saussure says,[56] 'from the reciprocal situation of the pieces of the language'. It is even more important than signification: 'what quantity of idea or phonic matter a sign contains is of less import than what there is around it in the other signs':[57] a prophetic sentence, if one realizes that it already was the foundation of Lévi-Strauss's homology and of the principle of taxonomies. Having thus carefully distinguished, with Saussure, signification and value, we immediately see that if we return to Hjelmslev's *strata* (substance and form), the signification partakes of the substance of the content, and value, of that of its form (*mutton* and *sheep* are in a paradigmatic relation *as signifieds* and not, of course, as signifiers).

II.5.2. *The articulation:* In order to account for the double phenomenon of signification and value, Saussure used the analogy of a sheet of paper: if we cut out shapes in it, on the one hand we get various pieces (A, B, C), each of which has a *value* in relation to its neighbours, and, on the other, each of these pieces has a recto and a verso *which have been cut out at the same time* (A—A', B—B', C—C'): this is the signification. This comparison is useful because it leads us to an original conception of the production of meaning: no longer as the mere correlation of a signifier and a signified, but perhaps more essentially *as an act of simultaneously cutting out* two amorphous masses, two 'floating kingdoms' as Saussure says. For Saussure imagines that at the (entirely theoretical) origin of meaning, ideas and sounds form two floating, labile, continuous and parallel masses of substances; meaning intervenes when one cuts at the same time and at a single stroke into these two masses. The signs (thus produced) are therefore *articuli;* meaning is therefore an order with chaos on either side, but this order is essentially a *division.* The language is an intermediate object between sound and thought: it consists *in uniting both while simultaneously decomposing them.* And Saussure suggests a new simile: signifier and signified are like two superimposed layers, one of air, the other of water; when the atmospheric pressure changes, the layer of water divides into waves: in the same way, the signifier is divided into *articuli*. These images, of the sheet of paper as well as of the waves, enable us to emphasize a fact which is of the utmost importance for the future of semiological analysis: that language is the domain of *articulations*, and the meaning is above all a cutting-out of shapes. It follows that the future task of semiology is far less to establish lexicons of objects than to rediscover the articulations which men impose on reality; looking into the distant and perhaps ideal future, we might say that semiology and taxonomy, although they are not yet born, are perhaps meant to be merged into a new science, arthrology, namely, the science of apportionment.

III. SYNTAGM AND SYSTEM

III.1. THE TWO AXES OF LANGUAGE

III.1.1. *Syntagmatic and associative relationships in linguistics:* For Saussure,[58] the relationships between linguistic terms can develop on two planes, each of which generates its own particular values; these two planes correspond to two forms of mental activity (this generalization was to be later adopted by Jakobson). The first plane is that of the *syntagms*; the syntagm is a combination of signs, which has space as a support. In the articulated language, this space is linear and irreversible (it is the 'spoken chain'): two elements cannot be pronounced at the same time (*re-enter, against all, human life*): each term here derives its value from its opposition to what precedes and what follows; in the chain of speech, the terms are really united *in praesentia*; the analytical activity which applies to the syntagm is that of carving out.

The second plane is that of the *associations* (if we still keep Saussure's terminology): 'Beside the discourse (syntagmatic plane), the units which have something in common are associated in memory and thus form groups within which various relationships can be found': *education* can be associated, through its meaning, to *upbringing* or *training*, and through its sound, to *educate*, *educator*, or to *application*, *vindication*. Each group forms a potential mnemonic series, a 'mnemonic treasure'; in each series, unlike what happens at the syntagmatic level, the terms are united *in absentia*; the analytic activity which applies to the associations is that of classification.

The syntagmatic and associative planes are united by a close relation, which Saussure has expressed by means of the following simile : each linguistic unit is like a column in a building of antiquity : this column is in a real relation of contiguity with other parts of the building, for instance the architrave (syntagmatic relation); but if this column is Doric, it evokes in us a comparison with other architectural orders, the Ionic or the Corinthian; and this is a potential relation of substitution (associative relation): the two planes are linked in such a way that the syntagm cannot 'progress' except by calling successively on new units taken from the associative plane. Since Saussure, the analysis of the associative plane has undergone considerable development; its very name has changed : we speak today, not of the associative, but of the *paradigmatic* plane,[59] or, as we shall henceforth do here, of the *systematic* plane. The associative plane has evidently a very close connection with 'the language' as a system, while the syntagm is nearer to speech. It is possible to use a subsidiary terminology : syntagmatic connections are *relations* in Hjelmslev, *contiguities* in Jakobson, *contrasts* in Martinet; systematic connections are *correlations* in Hjelmslev, *similarities* in Jakobsen, *oppositions* in Martinet.

III.1.2. *Metaphor and Metonymy in Jakobson:* Saussure had an intimation that the syntagmatic and the associative (that is, for us, the systematic) probably corresponded to two forms of mental activity, which meant an excursion outside linguistics. Jakobson, in a now famous text,[60] has adopted this extension by applying the opposition of the *metaphor* (of the systematic order) and the *metonymy* (of the syntagmatic order) to non-linguistic languages: there will therefore be 'discourses' of the metaphorical and of the metonymic types; it is obvious that neither type implies the exclusive use of one of the two models (since both syntagm and system are necessary to all discourse), but only implies the dominance of one of them. To the metaphoric order (in which the associations by substitution predominate) belong (according to Jakobson) the Russian lyrical songs, the works of Romanticism and of Symbolism, Surrealist painting, the films of Charlie Chaplin (in which the superimposed dissolves are equated by Jakobson to veritable filmic metaphors), the Freudian dream-symbols (by identification). To the metonymic order (in which the syntagmatic associations predominate) belong the heroic epics, the narratives of the Realist school, films by Griffith (close-ups, montage, and variations in the angles of the shots) and the oneiric projections by displacement or condensation. To Jakobson's enumeration could be added: on the side of metaphor, didactic expositions (which make use of definitions by substitution),[61] literary criticism of the thematic type, aphoristic types of discourse; on the side of metonymy, popular novels and newspaper narratives.[62] Let us note, following a remark by Jakobson, that the analyst (in the present instance, the semiologist) is better

equipped to speak about metaphor than about metonymy, because the metalanguage in which he must
conduct his analysis is itself metaphorical, and consequently homogeneous with the metaphor which
is its object: and indeed there is an abundant literature on metaphor, but next to nothing on metonymy.

III.1.3. *Semiological prospects:* The vistas Jakobson
opened by his remarks on the predominantly metaphorical and predominantly metonymic types of discourse show us the way towards a passage from
linguistics to semiology. For the two planes of the
articulated language must also exist in other significant systems. Although the units of the syntagm,
which result from a dividing operation, and the lists
of oppositions, which result from a classification, cannot be defined *a priori* but only as the outcome of a
general commutative test of the signifiers and the
signifieds, it is possible to indicate the plane of the
syntagm and that of the system in the case of a few
semiological systems without venturing as yet to
designate the syntagmatic units, or, therefore, the
paradigmatic variations to which they give rise (see
table, page 63). Such are the two axes of language,
and the main part of the semiological analysis consists in distributing the facts which have been listed
on each of these axes. It is logical to begin the work
with the syntagmatic division, since in principle this
is the operation which supplies the units which must
also be classified in paradigms; however, when confronted with an unknown system, it may be more
convenient to start from a few paradigmatic elements
empirically obtained, and to study the system before
the syntagm; but since we are here dealing with

theoretical Elements we shall keep to the logical order, which goes from the syntagm to the system.

III.2. THE SYNTAGM

III.2.1. *Syntagm and speech:* We have seen (I.1.6) that the nature of speech (in the Saussurean sense) was syntagmatic, since quite apart from the amplitude of phonation, it can be defined as a (varied) combination of (recurrent) signs: the spoken sentence is the very type of the syntagm; it is therefore certain that the syntagm has very close similarities to speech. Now for Saussure, there cannot be a linguistics of speech; is the linguistics of the syntagm consequently impossible? Saussure felt the difficulty and was careful to specify in what way the syntagm could not be considered as a speech phenomenon: firstly, because there exist fixed syntagms, which usage forbids us to alter in any way (*So what? Now then!*) and which are out of the reach of the combinative freedom of speech (these stereotyped syntagms therefore become sorts of paradigmatic units); secondly, because the syntagms of speech are constructed according to regular forms which thereby belong to the language (*unget-atable* is constructed after *unattainable, unforgivable,* etc.): there is, therefore, a *form* of the syntagm (in Hjelmslev's sense of the word) dealt with by *syntax* which is, so to speak, the 'glottic' version of the syntagm.[63] This does not alter the fact that the structural 'proximity' of the syntagm and of speech is an important fact: because it ceaselessly offers problems to be analysed, but also – conversely – because it enables a structural explanation to be

	System	*Syntagm*
Garment system	Set of pieces, parts or details which cannot be worn at the same time on the same part of the body, and whose variation corresponds to a change in the meaning of the clothing: toque – bonnet – hood, etc.	Juxtaposition in the same type of dress of different elements: skirt – blouse – jacket.
Food system	Set of foodstuffs which have affinities or differences, within which one chooses a dish in view of a certain meaning: the types of entrée, roast or sweet.	Real sequence of dishes chosen during a meal: this is the menu.
	A restaurant 'menu' actualizes both planes: the horizontal reading of the entrées, for instance, corresponds to the system, the vertical reading of the menu corresponds to the syntagm.	
Furniture system	Set of the 'stylistic' varieties of a single piece of furniture (a bed).	Juxtaposition of the different pieces of furniture in the same space: bed – wardrobe – table, etc.
Architecture system	Variations in style of a single element in a building, various types of roof, balcony, hall, etc.	Sequence of the details at the level of the whole building.

given of certain phenomena of 'naturalization' of connoted discourses. The close relation of syntagm and speech must therefore be kept carefully in mind.

III.2.2. *Discontinuity:* The syntagm presents itself in the form of a 'chain' (the flow of speech, for example). Now as we have seen (II.5.2), meaning can arise only from an articulation, that is, from a simultaneous division of the signifying layer, and the signified mass: language is, as it were, that which *divides* reality (for instance the continuous spectrum of the colours is verbally reduced to a series of discontinuous terms). Any syntagm therefore gives rise to an analytic problem: for it is at the same time continuous and yet cannot be the vehicle of a meaning unless it is articulated. How can we divide the syntagm? This problem arises again with every system of signs: in the articulated language, there have been innumerable discussions on the nature (that is, in fact, on the 'limits') of the word, and for certain semiological systems, we can here foresee important difficulties. True, there are rudimentary systems of strongly discontinuous signs, such as those of the Highway Code, which, for reasons of safety, must be radically different from each other in order to be immediately perceived; but the iconic syntagms, which are founded on a more or less analogical representation of a real scene, are infinitely more difficult to divide, and this is probably the reason for which these systems are almost always duplicated by articulated speech (such as the caption of a photograph) which endows them with the discontinuous aspect which they do not have. In spite of these difficulties, the division of the syntagm is a fundamental operation, since it must yield the paradigmatic units of the system; it is in fact the very definition of the syntagm, to be made of *a substance which must be carved up.*[64] The syntagm, when it takes the form of *speech*, appears as a 'text without end': how can one spot, in this text without end, the significant units, that is, the limits of the signs which constitute it?

III.2.3. *The commutation test:* In linguistics, the dividing up of the 'text without end' is done by means of the commutation test. This operative concept is already found in Trubetzkoy, but it has been established under its present name by Hjelmslev and Udall, .at the Fifth Congress of Phonetics in 1936. The commutation test consists of artificially introducing a change in the plane of expression (signifiers) and in observing whether this change brings about a correlative modification on the plane of content (signifieds). The point, in fact, is to create an artificial homology, that is to say a double paradigm, on one point of the 'text without end', in order to check whether the reciprocal substitution of two signifiers has as a consequence *ipso facto* the reciprocal substitution of two signifieds; if the commutation of two signifiers produces a commutation of the signifieds one is assured of having got hold, in the fragment of syntagm submitted to the text, of a syntagmatic unit: the first sign has been cut off from the mass. This operation can naturally be conducted reciprocally in starting from the signifieds: if, for instance, in a Greek substantive, the idea of 'two' is substituted for that of 'several', a change of expression is obtained and the change element is thereby obtained (mark of the dual, and mark of the plural). Certain changes, however, do not bring about any change in the opposite plane: Hjelmslev[65] therefore distinguishes the *commutation*, which generates a change of meaning (*poison/poisson*) from the *substitution*, which changes the expression, and not the content, and vice-versa (*bonjour/bonchour*). We must take note of the fact that the commutation is usually applied first to the plane of the signifiers, since it is the syntagm which has to be divided; one can resort to the signifieds, but this remains purely formal: the signified is not called upon for its own sake, by virtue of its 'substance', but merely as an index of the signifier: it *places* the signifier, that is all. In other words, in the ordinary commutation test, one calls into use the form of the signified (its oppositional value in relation to other signifieds), not its substance: 'The difference between the significations are of use, the significations themselves being without importance' (Belevitch).[66] The commutation test allows us in principle to spot, by degrees, the significant units which together weave the syntagm, thus preparing the classification of those units into paradigms; needless to say, it is possible in linguistics only because the analyst has some knowledge of the meaning of the tongue he analyses. But in semiology, we may come across systems whose meaning is unknown or uncertain: who can be sure that in passing from household bread to fine wheaten bread, or from toque to bonnet, we pass from one signified to another? In most cases, the semiologist will find here the relay of some institutions, some metalanguages, which will supply him with the signifieds which he needs for his commutations: the article on gastronomy or the fashion magazine (here again we find the advantage of non-isological systems);

otherwise, he will have to observe more patiently how consistently certain changes and certain recurrences are produced, like a linguist confronted with an unknown language.

III.2.4. *The syntagmatic units:* The commutation test in principle[67] supplies significant units, that is, fragments of syntagms endowed with a necessary sense; these are still for the time being syntagmatic units, since they are not yet classified: but it is certain that they are already also systematic units, since each one of them is a part of a potential paradigm:

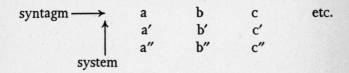

For the time being, we shall observe these units only from the syntagmatic point of view. In linguistics, the commutation test supplies a first type of unit: the *significant units,* each of which is endowed with a signifying facet and a signified facet (the monemes, or, using a more approximate term, the words, themselves compounded of lexemes and morphemes); but by reason of the double articulation of human language, a second commutation test, applied this time to the monemes, produces the appearance of a second type of unit: the *distinctive units* (phonemes).[68] These units have no meaning in themselves, but they nevertheless play their part in the production of meaning, since the commutation of one of them brings about a change of meaning for the moneme it is a part of (the commutation of a voiceless sign into a voiced sign brings about the passage of 'poisson' to 'poison').[69]

In semiology, it is impossible to guess in advance the syntagmatic units which analysis will discover for each system. We shall now be content with anticipating three kinds of problem. The first concerns the existence of complex systems which have combined syntagms as their starting point: a system of objects, like the food or the garment system, can be relayed by a linguistic system proper (the French tongue); we have in this case a garment- or a food-syntagm, and a written syntagm (the spoken chain) *directed towards* them (the dress or the menu recounted by the language): the units of both syntagms do not necessarily coincide: a unit of the food- or the garment-syntagm can be borne by a collection of written units. The second problem arises from the existence, in the semiological systems, of *sign-functions*, namely of signs born from a certain usage and in turn rationalized by it.[70] In opposition to the human language, in which the phonic substance is immediately significant, and only significant, most semiological systems probably involve a matter which has another function beside that of being significant (bread is used to nourish, garments to protect); we can therefore expect that in these systems the syntagmatic unit is composite and includes at least a support for the signification and a variant proper (*long/short skirt*). Finally, it is not out of the question that one might come across systems which are 'scattered', as it were, in which inert spaces of matter support here and there signs which are not only discontinuous but separate: the road-signs of the Highway Code, as found in real life, are separated by long stretches devoid of signification (fragments of roads or streets); one could then speak about syntagms which are (temporarily) dead.[71]

III.2.5 *The combinative constraints:* Once the syntagmatic units are defined for each system, there remains the task of finding the rules which determine their combination and arrangement along the syntagm; the monemes in language, the various garments in a given dress, the dishes in a menu, the road-signs along a street, succeed each other in an order which remains subject to certain constraints: the combination of the signs is free, but this freedom, which is what 'speech' means, remains under supervision (which is why, let it be stated once more, one must not confuse the syntagm with the syntax). In fact, the arrangement is the very condition of the syntagm: 'the syntagm is any set of hetero-functional signs; it is always (at least) binary, and its two terms are in a relation of reciprocal conditioning' (Mikus).[72] Several models of combinative constraints (that is, of the 'logic' of signs) can be imagined; we shall cite here, as examples, the three types of relation which, according to Hjelmslev, two syntagmatic units can enter into when they are contiguous: i) a relation of *solidarity*, when they necessarily imply each other; ii) of *simple implication*, when one implies the other without reciprocity; iii) of *combination*, when neither implies the other. The combinative constraints are fixed by the 'language', but 'speech' complies with them in varying degrees: there remains, therefore, some freedom in the association of syntagmatic units. As far as language is concerned, Jakobson has pointed out that the speaker enjoys, in combining linguistic units, a freedom which increases as he passes from the phoneme to the sentence: the freedom to construct paradigms of phonemes is nil, since the code is here established by the language; the freedom to group phonemes into monemes is limited, for there are 'laws' for governing the creation of words; the freedom to combine several 'words' into a sentence is real, although circumscribed by the syntax and in some cases by submission to certain stereotypes; the freedom to combine sentences is the greatest of all, for it no longer admits of constraints at the level of syntax (the constraints regarding the mental coherence of the discourse are no longer of a linguistic order).

Syntagmatic freedom is clearly related to certain *aleatory factors*: there are probabilities of saturation of certain syntactic forms by certain contents. The verb *to bark* can only be saturated by a reduced number of subjects; within a certain set of clothes, a skirt is unavoidably 'saturated' by a blouse, a sweater or a jacket, etc. This phenomenon is called *catalysis*; it is possible to imagine a purely formal lexicon which would provide, instead of the meaning of each word, the set of other words which could catalyse it according to possibilities which are of course variable – the smallest degree of probability would correspond to a 'poetic' zone of speech (Valle Inclan: 'Woe betide him who does not have the courage to join two words which had never been united').

III.2.6. *Identity and distance of syntagmatic units:* A remark by Saussure suggests that it is because signs recur that language is possible (cf. *supra* I.1.3.) Along the syntagmatic chain we do indeed find a certain number of identical units; the repetition of the signs is, however, corrected by *distance* phenomena between identical units. This problem leads us to statistical linguistics, or macro-linguistics, which is essentially a linguistics of the syntagm, without any reference to meaning. We have seen how near to speech the syntagm was: statistical linguistics is a linguistics of the various forms of speech (Lévi-Strauss). The syntagmatic distance of identical units is not, however, only a problem of macro-linguistics; this distance can be appreciated in stylistic terms (a repetition which occurs too soon being either aesthetically precluded or theoretically recommended) and then becomes an element of the connotative code.

III.3. THE SYSTEM

III.3.1. *Similarity and dissimilarity; difference:* The system constitutes the second axis of the language. Saussure has seen it in the shape of a series of associative fields, some determined by an affinity of sound (*education, saturation*), some by an affinity in meaning (*education, upbringing*). Each field is a store of potential terms (since only one of them is actualized in the present discourse): Saussure insists on the word *term* (he substitutes this for *word*, which is a syntagmatic unit), for, he says, 'as soon as we use "term" instead of "word", the idea of a system is brought to mind.'[73] Indeed, due attention paid to the system in the study of any set of signs practically always testifies to Saussurean influence; the school of Bloomfield, for instance, is reluctant to consider associative relations, while contrary to this, A. Martinet recommends the drawing of a clear distinction between the *contrasts* (relations of contiguity between syntagmatic units) and the *oppositions* (relations between the terms of the associative field).[74] The terms of the field (or paradigm) must at the same time be similar and dissimilar, include a common and a variable element: this is the case on the plane of the signifier, with *education* and *saturation*, and on the plane of the signified with *education* and *upbringing*.

This definition of the terms by means of an opposition seems simple; yet it raises an important theoretical problem. For the element which is common to all the terms of a paradigm (*-ation* in *education* and *saturation*) appears as a positive (non-differential) element, and this phenomenon seems to contradict the reiterated declarations by Saussure on the purely differential, oppositional nature of the language: 'In the language there are only differences without any positive terms'; 'Consider (the sounds) not as sounds having an absolute value, but a purely oppositional, relative, negative, value . . . In stating this, we must go much further, and consider every value in the language as oppositional and not as positive, absolute.'[75] And this, still by Saussure, and even more definite: 'It is a characteristic of the language, as of any semiological system in general, that it can admit no difference between what distinguishes a certain thing and what constitutes that thing.'[76] If, therefore, the language is purely differential, how can it include positive, non-differential elements? In fact, what seems the common element in a paradigm, is itself *elsewhere*, in another paradigm, that is, *according to* *another relevant factor*, a purely differential term: broadly speaking, in the opposition of *le* and *la, l* is indeed a common (positive) element, but in *le/ce*, it becomes a differential element: it is therefore relevance which, while limiting Saussure's statement, keeps it true;[77] the meaning still depends on an *aliud/aliud* relation, which keeps only the difference between two things.[78]

This configuration is questionable, however (whatever Saussure thought), in the semiological systems, in which the matter is not originally significant, and in which, consequently, the units comprise – probably – a positive part (which is the *support* of the signification) and a differential part, the variant; in a *short/long dress*, the vestimentary meaning pervades all the elements (which proves that we are really dealing with a significant unit), but the paradigm never applies to anything but the qualifying element (*long/short*) while the *dress* (support) does keep a positive value. The absolutely differential value of the language is therefore probable only if we mean the articulated language; in the secondary systems (which derive from non-significant usages), the language is 'impure', so to speak: it does contain a differential element (that is, pure 'language') at the level of the variants, but also something positive, at the level of the supports.

III.3.2. *The oppositions:* The internal arrangement of the terms in an associative or paradigmatic field is usually called – at least in linguistics, and more precisely, in phonology – an *opposition*. This is not a very good denomination, for on the one hand it presupposes too much the antonymic character of the

paradigmatic relation (Cantineau would have preferred *relation*, and Hjelmslev *correlation*), and on the
other hand, it seems to connote a binary relation,
about which there is no certainty that it is the foundation of all semiological paradigms. We shall, however, keep the word, since it is accepted.

The types of opposition are very varied, as we shall
see; but in its relations with the plane of content, an
opposition, whatever it may be, always appears as a
homology, as we have already indicated, apropos of
the commutation test: the 'leap' from one term of
the opposition to the other accompanies the 'leap'
from one signified to the other; it is to respect the
differential character of the system that one must
always think of the relation between signifier and
signified in terms, not simply of analogy, but of at
least a four-termed homology.

Besides, the 'leap' from one term to the other is
doubly alternating: the opposition between *bière* and
pierre, although very small (b/p), cannot be split into
indefinite intermediate states; an approximate sound
between b and p cannot in any way refer to an intermediate substance between *beer* and *stone*; there are
two parallel leaps: the opposition is still in the *all-
or-nothing* category. We again find the principle of
difference which is the foundation of opposition: it
is this principle which must inspire the analysis of the
associative sphere; for to deal with the opposition can
only mean to observe the relations of similarity or
difference which may exist between the terms of the
oppositions, that is, quite precisely, to classify them.

III.3.3. *The classification of oppositions:* We know
that since human language is doubly articulated, it

comprises two sorts of opposition: the distinctive oppositions (between phonemes), and the significant oppositions (between monemes). Trubetzkoy has suggested a classification of the distinctive oppositions, which J. Cantineau has tried to adopt and extend to the significant oppositions in the language. As at the first glance semiological units are nearer to the semantic units of the language than to its phonological units, we shall give here Cantineau's classification, for even if it cannot be easily applied (subsequently) to the semiological oppositions, it has the advantage of bringing to our notice the main problems posed by the structure of oppositions.[79] At first sight when one passes from a phonological to a semantic system, the oppositions in the latter are innumerable, since each signifier seems to be opposed to all the others; a principle of classification is possible, however, if one chooses as a guide *a typology of the relations between the similar element and the dissimilar element of the opposition*. Thus Cantineau obtains the following types of opposition – which can also be combined with each other.[80]

A. *Oppositions classified according to their relations with the whole of the system*

A.1. *Bilateral and multilateral oppositions*. In these oppositions, the common element between two terms, or 'basis for comparison', is not found in any of the other oppositions of the code (*bilateral oppositions*) or, on the contrary, is found in other oppositions of the code (*multilateral oppositions*). Let us take the written Latin alphabet: the opposition of the figures E/F is bilateral, because the common elt F is not found again in any other letter;[81] on the contrary, the opposition P/R is multilateral, for the P shape (or common element) is again found in B.

A.2. *Proportional and isolated oppositions*. In these oppositions, the difference is constituted into a sort of model. Thus: *Mann/Männer* and *Land/Länder* are proportional oppositions; in the same way: (*nous*) *disons/*(*vous*) *dites* and (*nous*) *faisons/*(*vous*) *faites*. The oppositions which are not proportional are isolated; they are evidently the most numerous. In semantics, only grammatical (morphological) oppositions are proportional; the lexical oppositions are isolated.

B. *Oppositions classified according to the relation between the terms of the oppositions*

B.1. *Privative oppositions*. These are the best known. A privative opposition means any opposition in which the signifier of a term is characterized by the presence of a significant element, or *mark*, which is missing in the signifier of the other. This is therefore the general opposition *marked/unmarked: mange* (without any indication of the person or number): unmarked term; *mangeons* (first person of the plural): marked term. This disposition corresponds in logic to the relation of inclusion. We shall mention in this connection two important problems. The first concerns the *mark*. Some linguists have identified the mark with the exceptional and have invoked a feeling for the normal in order to decide which terms are *unmarked*; according to them, the *unmarked* is what is frequent or banal, or else derived from the *marked* by a subsequent subtraction. Thus is reached

the idea of a negative mark (that which is subtracted) :
for the unmarked terms are more numerous in the
language than the marked ones (Trubetzkoy, Zipf).
Thus Cantineau considers that *rond* is marked, in relation to *ronde*, which is not; but this is in fact because Cantineau appeals to the content, according to
which the masculine is marked in relation to the
feminine. For Martinet, on the contrary, the mark is
literally an *additional* significant element; this does
not prevent in any way, in the case of *masculine/
feminine*, the parallelism which normally exists between the mark of the signifier and that of the
signified, for 'masculine' in fact corresponds to a non-
differentiation between the sexes, to a kind of
abstract generality (il fait *beau*, on est *venu*), as opposed to which, the feminine is well marked; a
semantic mark and a formal mark go well together :
when one wants to say more, one adds a supplementary sign.[82]

The second problem arising in connection with
privative opposition is that of the unmarked term.
It is called the *zero degree* of the opposition. The zero
degree is therefore not a total absence (this is a
common mistake), *it is a significant absence*. We have
here a pure differential state; the zero degree testifies
to the power held by any system of signs, of creating
meaning 'out of nothing' : 'the language can be content with an opposition of something and nothing.'[83]
The concept of the zero degree, which sprang from
phonology, lends itself to a great many applications :
in semantics, in which *zero signs* are known ('a "zero
sign" is spoken of in cases where the absence of any
explicit signifier functions by itself as a signifier');[84]
in logic ('A is in the zero state, that is to say that A

77

does not actually exist, but under certain conditions it can be made to appear');[85] in ethnology, where Lévi-Strauss could compare the notion of mana to it ('. . . the proper function of the zero phoneme is to be opposed to the absence of the phoneme . . . Similarly, it could be said . . . that the function of notions of the "mana" type is to be opposed to the absence of signification without involving in itself any particular signification');[86] finally, in rhetoric, where, carried on to the connotative plane, the absence of rhetorical signifiers constitutes in its turn a stylistic signifier.[87]

B.2. *Equipollent oppositions.* In these oppositions, whose relation would in logic be a relation of exteriority, the two terms are equivalent, that is to say that they cannot be considered as the negation and the affirmation of a peculiarity (privative oppositions): in *foot/feet*, there is neither mark nor absence of mark. These oppositions are semantically the most numerous, even if the language, for economy's sake, often attempts to replace equipollent oppositions by privative oppositions: first, because in the latter the relation between similarity and dissimilarity is well balanced, and second, because they enable us to build proportional series such as *poet/poetess, count/countess*, etc., whereas *stallion/mare*, which is an equipollent opposition, has no derivation.[88]

C. *Oppositions classified according to the extent of their differentiating value*

C.1. *Constant oppositions.* This is the case of the signifieds which *always* have different signifiers: *(je) mange/(nous) mangeons*; the first person of the singular and that of the plural have different signifiers, in French, in all verbs, tenses and modes.

C.2. *Oppositions which can be eliminated or neutralized.* This is the case of the signifieds which do not always have different signifiers, so that the two terms of the opposition can sometimes be identical: to the semantic opposition *third person singular/third person plural*, there correspond signifiers which are at one time different (*finit/finissent*), at others phonetically identical (*mange/mangent*).

III.3.4. *Semiological oppositions:* What may become of these types of opposition in semiology? It is naturally much too early to tell, for the paradigmatic plane of a new system cannot be analysed without a broad inventory. Nothing proves that the types laid down by Trubetzkoy and partly[89] adopted by Cantineau could concern systems other than language: new types of opposition are conceivable, especially if one is prepared to depart from the binary model. We shall, however, attempt to sketch here a confrontation between the types of Trubetzkoy and Cantineau and what can be known about two very different semiological systems: the Highway Code and the fashion system.

In the Highway Code we shall find multilateral proportional oppositions (for instance, all those which are built on a variation of colour within the opposition of circle and triangle), private oppositions (when an added mark makes the meaning of a circle vary, for instance) and constant oppositions (the signifieds always have different signifiers), but neither equipollent nor suppressible oppositions. This economy is understandable: the Highway Code must be immediately and unambiguously legible if it is to prevent accidents; therefore it eliminates those oppositions which need the longest time to be understood, either because they are not reducible to proper paradigms (equipollent oppositions) or because they offer a choice of two signifieds for a single signifier (suppressible oppositions).

On the contrary, in the fashion system,[90] which tends to polysemy, we encounter all types of opposition, except, of course, bilateral and constant oppositions, whose effect would be to increase the particularity and the rigidity of the system.

Semiology, in the proper sense of the word, that is, as a science comprising all systems of signs, will therefore be able to make good use of the general distribution of the types of opposition throughout the various systems – an observation which would have no object at the level of the language only. But above all, the extension of semiological research will probably lead to the study (which may eventually prove fruitless) of serial, and not only oppositional, paradigmatic relations; for it is not certain that, once confronted with complex objects, deeply involved in some matter and in various usages, one will be able to reduce the functioning of the meaning to the alternative of two polar elements or to the opposition of a mark and a zero degree. This leads us to remind the reader once more that the most vexed question connected with paradigms is that of the binary principle.

III.3.5. *Binarism:* The importance and the simplicity of the privative opposition (*marked/unmarked*), which is by definition an alternative, have led to the question whether all known oppositions should not be reduced to the binary pattern (that is, based on the presence or absence of a mark), in other words, whether the binary principle did not reflect a universal fact; and on the other hand, whether, being universal, it might not have a natural foundation.

About the first point, it is certain that binary patterns are very frequently encountered. It is a principle which has been acknowledged for centuries, that information can be transmitted by means of a binary code, and most of the artificial codes which have been invented by very different societies have been binary, from the 'bush telegraph' (and notably the *talking drum* of the Congo tribes, which has two notes) to the morse alphabet and the contemporary developments of 'digitalism', or alternative codes with 'digits' in computers and cybernetics. However, if we leave the plane of the 'logo-techniques', to come back to that of the systems which are not artificial, which concerns us here, the universality of the binary principle appears far less certain. Paradoxically, Saussure himself never did conceive the associative field as binary: for him, the terms of a field are neither finite in number, nor determined in their order: [91] 'A term is like the centre of a constellation, the point where other co-ordinate terms, the sum of which is indefinite, converge.' [92] The only restriction imposed by Saussure concerns the flexional paradigms, which of course are finite series. It is phonology which has focused attention on the binarism of language (only at the level of the second articulation, it is true); is this binarism absolute? Jakobson thinks so: [93] according to him, the phonetic systems of all languages could be described by means of a dozen distinctive features, all of them binary, that is to say, either present or absent, or, as the case may be, irrelevant. This binary universalism has been questioned and qualified by Martinet:[94] binary oppositions are the majority, not the totality; the universality of binarism is not certain. Questioned in phonology, unexplored in semantics, binarism is the great unknown in semiology, whose types of opposition have not yet been outlined. To account for complex oppositions, one can of course resort to the model brought to light by linguistics, and which consists in a 'complicated' alternative, or four-termed opposition : two polarized terms (*this or that*), a mixed term (*this and that*) and a neutral term (*neither this nor that*); these oppositions, although they are more flexible than the privative oppositions, will probably not save us from having to pose the problem of the *serial*, and not only oppositive, paradigms: the universality of binarism is not yet founded.

Nor is its 'naturalness' (and this is the second point in which it lays itself open to discussion). It is very tempting to found the general binarism of the codes on physiological data, inasmuch as it is likely that neuro-cerebral perception also functions in an all-or-nothing way, and particularly sight and hearing, which seem to work by means of a review of alternatives.[95] Thus would be elaborated, from nature to society, a vast, 'digital', not 'analogical', translation of the world; but nothing of all this is certain. In fact, and to conclude briefly on the question of binarism, we may wonder whether this is not a classification which is both necessary and transitory : in which case binarism also would be a metalanguage, a particular taxonomy meant to be swept away by history, after having been true to it for a moment.

III.3.6. *Neutralization:* In order to finish with the principal phenomena pertaining to the system, a word has to be said about *neutralization*. This term means in linguistics the phenomenon whereby a relevant opposition loses its relevance, that is, ceases to be significant. In general, the neutralization of a systematic opposition occurs in response to the context: it is therefore the syntagm which cancels out the system, so to speak. In phonology, for instance, the opposition between two phonemes can be nullified as a consequence of the position of one of the terms in the spoken chain: in French, there is normally an opposition between *é* and *è* when one of these terms is at the end of a word (*j'aimai/j'aimais*); this opposition ceases to be relevant anywhere else: it is neutralized. Conversely, the relevant opposition *ó/ò* (*saute/sotte*) is neutralized at the end of a word, where one finds only the sound *ó* (*pot, mot, eau*). In this case the two neutralized features are reunited under a single sound which is called *archiphoneme*, and which is written with a capital letter: *é/è*=E; *ó/ò*=O.

In semantics, neutralization has been the object of only a few soundings since the semantic 'system' is not yet established: J. Dubois[96] has observed that a semantic unit can lose its relevant features in certain syntagms; around 1872, in phrases such as: *emancipation of the workers, emancipation of the masses, emancipation of the proletariat,* both parts of the phrase can be commuted without altering the meaning of the complex semiology unit.

In semiology, we must once more wait for a certain number of systems to be reconstructed before outlining a theory of neutralization. Some systems will perhaps radically exclude the phenomenon : by reason of its very purpose, which is the immediate and un-ambiguous understanding of a small number of signs, the Highway Code cannot tolerate any neutraliza-tion. Fashion, on the contrary, which has polysemic (and even pansemic) tendencies, admits numerous neutralizations: whereas in one case *chandail* refers back to the seaside, and *sweater* to the mountains, in another case it will be possible to speak of a *chandail ou un sweater* for the seaside; the relevance *chandail/ sweater* is lost:[97] the two pieces are absorbed into a kind of 'archi-vesteme' of the 'woollen' type. We may say, at least as far as the semiological hypothesis is concerned (that is, when we disregard the problems raised by the second articulation, that of the purely distinctive units), that there is a neutralization when two signifiers fall under the heading of a single signi-fied, or vice-versa (for it will also be possible for the signifieds to be neutralized).

Two useful notions must be mentioned in connec-tion with this phenomenon. The first is that of the *field of dispersal* or *security margin*. The dispersal field is made up of the varieties in execution of a unit (of a phoneme, for instance) as long as these varieties do not result in an alteration in meaning (that is, as long as they do not become relevant varia-tions); the 'edges' of the dispersal field are its margins of security. This is a notion which is not very useful in dealing with a system in which the 'language' is very strong (in the car system, for instance), but valu-able when a rich 'speech' multiplies the opportunities for difference in execution: in the food system, for instance, we can speak of the dispersal field of a dish, which will be established by the limits within which this dish remains significant, whatever 'frills' the performer brings into its preparation.

Here is the second notion : the varieties which make up the dispersal field are sometimes called *combinative variants* when they depend on the combination of signs, that is, on the immediate context (the *d* of *nada* and that of *fonda* are not identical, but the variation does not affect the meaning), sometimes *individual* or *optional* variants. In French, for instance, whether you are a native of Burgundy or Paris, that is to say whether you use a rolled or uvular *r*, you are understood just the same. The combinative variants have long been considered as phenomena pertaining to speech; they certainly are very close to it, but are nowadays held to pertain to the language, since they are 'compulsory'. It is probable that in semiology, where studies on connotation are likely to be important, the combinative variations will become a central notion : for variants which are non-significant on the plane of denotation (for instance the rolled and the uvular *r*) can become significant on the plane of connotation, and from being combinative variants they refer now to two different signifieds : in the language of the theatre, one will signify 'the Burgundian', the other 'the Parisian', without ceasing to be nonsignificant in the denotative system.

Such are the first implications of neutralization. In a very general way, neutralization represents a sort of pressure of the syntagm on the system, and we know that the syntagm, which is close to speech, is to a certain extent a factor of 'defaulting'; the strongest systems (like the Highway Code) have poor syntagms; the great syntagmatic complexes (like the image system) tend to make the meaning ambiguous.

III.3.7. *Transgressions:* Syntagm system : such are the two planes of language. Now, although such studies are only to be found here and there in a sketchy way, we must foresee the future exhaustive exploration of the whole of the phenomena in which one plane overlaps the other, in a way which is 'teratological', so to speak, compared to the normal relations of the system and the syntagm. For the mode of articulation of the two axes is sometimes 'perverted', when for instance a paradigm is extended into a syntagm. There is then a defiance of the usual distribution *syntagm/system,* and it is probably around this transgression that a great number of creative phenomena are situated, as if perhaps there were here a junction between the field of aesthetics and the defections from the semantic system. The chief transgression is obviously the extension of a paradigm on to the syntagmatic plane, since normally only one term of the operation is actualized, the other (or others) remaining potential : this is what would happen, broadly speaking, if one attempted to elaborate a discourse by putting one after the other all the terms of the same declension. The question of these syntagmatic extensions had already arisen in phonology, where Trnka, corrected in many respects by Trubetzkoy, had posited that within a morpheme, two paradigmatic terms of a correlative couple cannot occur side by side.

But it is evidently in semantics that normality (to which Trnka's law refers in phonology) and the departures from it have the greatest interest, since we are there on the plane of significant (and no longer distinctive) units, and since the overlapping of the axes of language brings about an apparent alteration in the meaning. Here are, from this point of view, three directions which will have to be explored.

In face of the classical oppositions or oppositions of *presence*, J. Tubiana[98] suggests the acknowledgment of oppositions of *arrangement* : two words exhibit the same features, but the arrangement of these features differs in both : *rame/mare*; *dur/rude*; *charme/marche*. These oppositions form the majority of plays on words, puns and spoonerisms. In fact, starting from a relevant opposition, (*Félibres/fébriles*), it is sufficient to remove the stroke which indicates the paradigmatic opposition to obtain a strange-sounding syntagm (a newspaper has in fact used *Félibres fébriles* as a title); this sudden suppression of the stroke is rather reminiscent of the removal of a kind of structural censorship, and one cannot fail to connect this phenomenon with that of dreams as producers or explorers of puns.[99]

Another direction which has to be explored, and an important one, is that of rhyme. Rhyming produces an associative sphere at the level of sound, that is to say, of the signifiers : there are paradigms of rhymes. In relation to these paradigms, the rhymed discourse is clearly made of a fragment of the system extended into a syntagm. According to this, rhyming coincides with a transgression of the law of the distance between the syntagm and the system (Trnka's law); it corresponds to a deliberately created tension between the congenial and the dissimilar, to a kind of structural scandal.

Finally, rhetoric as a whole will no doubt prove to

be the domain of these creative transgressions; if we remember Jakobson's distinction, we shall understand that any metaphoric series is a syntagmatized paradigm, and any metonymy a syntagm which is frozen and absorbed in a system; in metaphor, selection becomes contiguity, and in metonymy, contiguity becomes a field to select from. It therefore seems that it is always on the frontiers of the two planes that creation has a chance to occur.

IV. DENOTATION AND CONNOTATION

IV.1. STAGGERED SYSTEMS

It will be remembered that any system of signifi-cations comprises a plane of expression (E) and a plane of content (C) and that the signification co-incides with the relation (R) of the two planes: E R C. Let us now suppose that such a system E R C becomes in its turn a mere element of a second system, which thus is more extensive than the first: we then deal with two systems of significations which are imbri-cated but are out of joint with each other, or stag-gered. But this derivation can occur in two entirely different ways dependent upon the point of insertion of the first system into the second, and therefore it can result in two opposite sets.

In the first case, *the first system (ERC) becomes the plane of expression, or signifier, of the second system:*

$$
\begin{array}{c|ccc}
2 & \overbrace{E} & R & C \\
1 & E\,R\,C & &
\end{array}
$$

or else: (ERC) RC. This is the case which Hjelmslev calls *connotative semiotics;* the first system is then the plane of *denotation* and the second system (wider than the first) the plane of *connotation.* We shall therefore say that *a connoted system is a system whose plane of expression is itself constituted by a signifying system:* the common cases of connotation will of course consist of complex systems of which language forms the first system (this is, for instance, the case with literature).

In the second (opposite) case of derivation, *the first system (ERC) becomes, not the plane of expression, as in connotation, but the plane of content, or signified, of the second system* =

$$
\begin{array}{cccc}
2 & E & R & C \\
1 & & & \overbrace{E\ R\ C}
\end{array}
$$

or else: E R (ERC). This is the case with all *metalanguages*: *a metalanguage is a system whose plane of content is itself constituted by a signifying system; or else, it is a semiotics which treats of a semiotics.*

Such are the two ways of amplification of double systems:

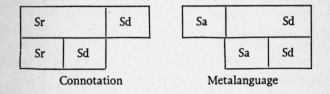

Connotation   Metalanguage

IV.2. CONNOTATION

Connotative phenomena have not yet been systematically studied (a few indications will be found in Hjelmslev's *Prolegomena*). Yet the future probably belongs to a linguistics of connotation, for society continually develops, from the first system which human language supplies to it, second-order significant systems, and this elaboration, now proclaimed and now disguised, is very close to a real historical anthropolgy. Connotation, being itself a system, comprises signifiers, signifieds, and the process which unites the former to the latter (signification), and it is the inventory of these three elements which one should undertake in the first place for each system.

The signifiers of connotation, which we shall call *connotators*, are made up of *signs* (signifiers and signifieds united) of the denoted system. Naturally, several denoted signs can be grouped together to form a single connotator – provided the latter has a single signified of connotation; in other words, the units of the connoted system do not necessarily have the same size as those of the denoted system : large fragments of the denoted discourse can constitute a single unit of the connoted system (this is the case, for instance, with the tone of a text, which is made up of numerous words, but which nevertheless refers to a single signified). Whatever the manner in which it 'caps' the denoted message, connotation does not exhaust it : there always remains 'something denoted' (otherwise the discourse would not be possible) and the connotators are always in the last analysis discontinuous and scattered signs, naturalized by the denoted language which carries them.

As for the signified of connotation, its character is at once general, global and diffuse; it is, if you like, a fragment of ideology : the sum of the messages in French refers, for instance, to the signified 'French'; a book can refer to the signified 'Literature'. These signifieds have a very close communication with culture, knowledge, history, and it is through them, so to speak, that the environmental world invades the system. We might say that *ideology* is the *form* (in Hjelmslev's sense of the word) of the signifieds of connotation, while *rhetoric* is the form of the connotators.

IV.3. METALANGUAGE

In connotative semiotics, the signifiers of the second system are constituted by the signs of the first; this is reversed in metalanguage: there the signifieds of the second system are constituted by the signs of the first. Hjelmslev has made the notion of metalanguage explicit in the following way: it being understood that an *operation* is a *description* founded on the empirical principle, that is to say non-contradictory (coherent), exhaustive and simple, scientific semiotics, or metalanguage, is an operation, whereas connotative semiotics is not. It is evident that semiology, for instance, is a metalanguage, since as a second-order system it takes over a first language (or language-object) which is the system under scrutiny; and this system-object is *signified* through the metalanguage of semiology. The notion of metalanguage must not be confined to scientific languages; when ordinary language, *in its denoted state*, takes over a system of signifying objects, it becomes an 'operation', that is, a metalanguage. This is the case, for instance, with the fashion magazine which 'speaks' the significations of garments, just as one speaks a language; this, however, is only ideally speaking, for magazines do not usually exhibit a purely denoted discourse, so that eventually we deal here with a complex ensemble, where language, at its denoted level, is a metalanguage, but where this metalanguage is in its turn caught up in a process of connotation :

3 Connotation	Sr : rhetoric	Sd = ideology
2 Denotation : Metalanguage	Sr	Sd
1 Real System	Sr	Sd

IV.4. CONNOTATION AND METALANGUAGE

Nothing in principle prevents a metalanguage from becoming in its turn the language-object of a new metalanguage; this would, for example, be the case with semiology if it were to be 'spoken' by another science. If one agreed to define the social sciences as coherent, exhaustive and simple languages (Hjelmslev's empirical principle), that is as *operations*, each new science would then appear as a new language which would have as its object the metalanguage which precedes it, while being directed towards the reality-object which is at the root of these 'descriptions'; the history of the social sciences would thus be, in a sense, a diachrony of metalanguages, and each science, including of course semiology, would contain the seeds of its own death, in the shape of the language destined to speak it. This relativity, which is an inherent part of the general system of metalanguages, allows us to qualify the image which we might at first form, of a semiologist over-confident in the face of connotation; the whole of a semiological analysis usually requires, in addition to the studied system and the (denoted) language which in most cases takes it over, a system of connotation and the metalanguage of the analysis which is applied to it. We might say that society, which holds the plane of connotation, speaks the signifiers of the system considered, while the semiologist speaks its signifieds; he therefore seems to have the objective function of decipherer (his language is an operation) in relation to the world which naturalizes or conceals the signs of the first system under the signifiers of the second; but his objectivity is made provisional by the very history which renews metalanguages.

CONCLUSION: SEMIOLOGICAL RESEARCH

The aim of semiological research is to reconstitute the functioning of the systems of significations other than language in accordance with the process typical of any structuralist activity, which is to build a *simulacrum* of the objects under observation.[100] To undertake this research, it is necessary frankly to accept from the beginning (and especially at the beginning) a limiting principle. This principle, which once more we owe to linguistics, is the principle of relevance:[101] it is decided to describe the facts which have been gathered *from one point of view only*, and consequently to keep, from the heterogeneous mass of these facts, only the features associated with this point of view, to the exclusion of any others (these features are said to be *relevant*). The phonologist, for instance, examines sounds only from the point of view of the meaning which they produce without concerning himself with their physical, articulated nature; the relevance chosen by semiological research centres by definition round the signification of the objects analysed: these are examined only in relation to the meaning which is theirs, without bringing in — at least prematurely, that is, before the system is reconstituted as far as possible — the other determining factors of these objects (whether psychological, sociological or physical). These other factors must of course not be denied – they each are ascribable to another type of relevance; but they must themselves be treated in semiological terms, that is to say that their place and their function in the system of meaning must be determined. Fashion, for instance, evidently has economic and sociological implications; but the semiologist will treat neither the economics nor the sociology of fashion : he will only say at which level of the semantic system of fashion economics and sociology acquire semiological relevance : at the level of the vestmentary sign, for instance, or at that of the associative constraints (taboos), or at that of the discourse of connotation.

The principle of relevance evidently has as a consequence for the analyst a situation of *immanence* : one observes a given system *from the inside*. Since, however, the limits of the system which is the object of the research are not known in advance (the object being precisely to reconstitute this system), the *immanence* can only apply at the beginning to a heterogeneous set of facts which will have to be processed for their structure to be known : this is the *corpus*. The corpus is a finite collection of materials, which is determined in advance by the analyst, with some (inevitable) arbitrariness, and on which he is going to work. For instance, if one wishes to reconstitute the food system of the French of today, one will have to decide in advance which body of documents the analysis will deal with (menus found in magazines? restaurant menus? menus observed in real life? menus passed on by word of mouth?), and once this corpus has been defined, one will have to keep to it : that is to say, on the one hand not add anything to it during the course of the research, but also exhaust it completely by analysis, every fact included in the corpus having to be found in the system.

How should one choose the corpus on which one is going to work? This obviously depends on the suspected nature of the system: a corpus of facts concerning food cannot be submitted to the same criteria of choice as a corpus of car models. We can only venture here two general recommendations.

First, the corpus must be wide enough to give reasonable hope that its elements will saturate a complete system of resemblances and differences; it is certain that when one goes through a collection of data, after a time one eventually comes across facts and relations which have already been noticed (we have seen that an identity of signs is a phenomenon pertaining to the language); these 'returns' are more and more frequent, until one no longer discovers any new material: the corpus is then saturated.

Second, the corpus must be as homogeneous as possible. To begin with, homogeneous in substance: there is an obvious interest in working on materials constituted by one and the same substance, like the linguist who deals only with the phonic substance; in the same way, ideally, a good corpus of documents on the food system should comprise only one and the same type of document (restaurant menus, for instance). Reality, however, most commonly presents mixed substances; for instance, garments and written language in fashion; images, music and speech in films, etc; it will therefore be necessary to accept heterogeneous corpuses, but to see to it, in that case, that one makes a careful study of the systematic articulation of the substances concerned (and chiefly, that one pays due attention to separating the real from the language which takes it over), that is, that one gives to their very heterogeneity a structural interpretation.

Further, homogeneous in time: in principle, the corpus must eliminate diachronic elements to the utmost; it must coincide with a state of the system, a cross-section of history. Without here entering into the theoretical debate between synchrony and diachrony, we shall only say that, from an operative point of view, the corpus must keep as close as possible to the synchronic sets. A varied but temporally limited corpus will therefore be preferable to a narrow corpus stretched over a length of time, and if one studies press phenomena, for instance, a sample of newspapers which appeared at the same time will be preferable to the run of a single paper over several years. Some systems establish their own synchrony of their own accord — fashion, for instance, which changes every year; but for the others one must choose a short period of time, even if one has to complete one's research by taking soundings in the diachrony. These initial choices are purely operative and inevitably in part arbitrary: it is impossible to guess the speed at which systems will alter, since the essential aim of semiological research (that is, what will be found last of all) may be precisely to discover the systems' own particular time, the history of forms.

NOTES

[1] 'A concept is assuredly not a thing, but neither is it merely the consciousness of a concept. A concept is an instrument and a history, that is, a bundle of possibilities and obstacles involved in the world as experienced.' (G. G. Granger, *Méthodologie économique*, p. 23.)

[2] A danger stressed by C. Lévi-Strauss, *Anthropologie structurale*, p. 58. *Structural Anthropology*, tr. by Claire Jacobson and Brooke Grundfest Schoepf (Basic Books, New York and London, 1963), pp. 47–8.

[3] This feature has been noted (with misgiving) by M. Cohen ('Linguistique moderne et idéalisme', in *Recherches internationales*, May 1958, no. 7).

[4] It should be noted that the first definition of the language (*langue*) is taxonomic: it is a principle of classification.

[5] Cf. *infra*, II.5.1.

[6] *Acta linguistica*, I, 1, p. 5.

[7] L. Hjelmslev: *Essais Linguistiques* (Copenhagen, 1959), pp. 69 ff.

[8] Cf. *infra*, II.1.3.

[9] Cf. *infra*, II.1.3.

[10] 'La mécanique de l'analyse quantitative en linguistique', in *Études de linguistique appliquée*, 2, Didier, p. 37.

[11] A. Martinet: *Éléments de linguistique générale* (Armand Colin, 1960), p. 30. *Elements of General Linguistics*, tr. by Elizabeth Palmer (Faber & Faber, 1964), pp. 33–4.

[12] Cf. *infra* on the syntagm, Ch. III.

[13] Saussure, in R. Godel, *Les sources manuscrites du Cours de Linguistique générale* (Droz, Minard, 1957), p. 90.

[14] Cf. *infra*, Ch. IV.

[15] R. Jakobson, 'Deux aspects du langage et deux types d'aphasies', in *Essais de Linguistique générale* (Éditions de Minuit), 1963, p. 54. This is the second part of *Fundamentals of Language* (R. Jakobson and M. Halle, The Hague, 1956). C. L. Ebeling, *Linguistic units* (Mouton, The Hague, 1960), p. 9.

NOTES

A. Martinet, *A functional view of language* (Oxford, Clarendon Press, 1962), p. 105.

[16] *Writing Degree Zero.*

[17] *Essais de Linguistique générale*, Chapter 9. This is a translation of *Shifters, verbal categories and the Russian verb* (Russian Language Project, Department of Slavic Languages and Literature, Harvard University, 1957).

[18] W. Doroszewski, 'Langue et Parole', *Odbitka z Prac Filogisznych*, XLV (Warsaw, 1930), pp. 485–97.

[19] M. Merleau-Ponty, *Phénoménologie de la Perception*, 1945, p. 229. *Phenomenology of Perception*, tr. by Colin Smith. (Routledge & Kegan Paul, in conjunction with the Humanities Press, New York, 1962), pp. 196–7.

[20] M. Merleau-Ponty, *Eloge de la Philosophie* (Gallimard, 1953).

[21] G. Granger, 'Evènement et structure dans les sciences de l'homme', in *Cahiers de l'Institut de science économique appliquée*, no. 55, May 1957.

[22] See F. Braudel, 'Histoire et sciences sociales: la longue durée', in *Annales*, Oct.–Dec. 1958.

[23] *Anthropologie Structurale*, p. 230 (*Structural Anthropology*, pp. 208–9), and 'Les mathématiques de l'homme', in *Esprit*, Oct. 1956.

[24] 'There never is any premeditation, or even any meditation, or reflection on forms, outside the act, the occasion of speech, except an unconscious, non-creative activity: that of classifying' (Saussure, in Godel, op. cit., p. 58).

[25] *Principes de Phonologie* (tr. by J. Cantineau, 1957 ed.). p. 19.

[26] Cf. *infra*, Ch. IV.

[27] Cf. *infra*, II.4.3.

[28] J. P. Charlier: 'La notion de signe ($\sigma\eta\mu\epsilon\tilde{\iota}o\nu$) dans le IVè évangile', in *Revue des sciences philosophiques et théologiques*, 1959, 43, no. 3, pp. 434–48.

[29] This was very clearly expressed by St Augustine: 'A sign is something which, in addition to the substance absorbed by the senses, calls to mind of itself some other thing'.

[30] Cf. the shifters and the indicial symbols, *supra*, I.1.8.

[31] H. Wallon, *De l'acte à la pensée*, 1942, pp. 175–250.

[32] Although very rudimentary, the analysis given here, *supra*, II.1.1, concerns the *form* of the following signifieds: *sign, symbol, index, signal.*

[33] The case of the pictorial image should be set aside, for the image is immediately communicative, if not significant.

[34] Cf. R. Barthes: 'A propos de deux ouvrages récents de Cl. Lévi-Strauss: Sociologie et Socio-Logique', in *Information sur les sciences sociales* (UNESCO), Vol. 1, no. 4, Dec. 1962, pp. 114–22.

[35] Cf. *infra*, II.4.2.

[36] This discussion was taken up again by Borgeaud, Bröcker and Lohmann, in *Acta linguistica*, III.1.27.

[37] R. Hallig and W. von Wartburg, *Begriffssystem als Grundlage für die Lexicographie* (Berlin, Akademie Verlag, 1952), XXV.

[38] The bibliography of Trier and Matoré will be found in P. Guiraud, *La Sémantique*, P.U.F. ('Que sais-je?'), pp. 70 ff.

[39] This is what we have attempted to do here for *sign* and *symbol* (*supra*, II.1.1.).

[40] These examples are given by G. Mounin: 'Les analyses sémantiques', in *Cahiers de l'Institut de science économique appliquée*, March 1962, no. 123.

[41] It would be advisable henceforth to adopt the distinction suggested by A. J. Greimas: *semantic* = referring to the content; *semiological* = referring to the expression.

[42] Cf. R. Francès, *La perception de la musique* (Vrin, 1958), 3rd part.

[43] Cf. *infra*, III.2.3.

[44] Cf. *infra*, *Ch. III* (Syntagm and system).

[45] Cf. *infra*, II.5.2.

[46] Cf. R. Ortigues, *Le discours et le symbole* (Aubier, 1962).

[47] Cf. *infra*, Ch. IV.

[48] J. Laplanche et S. Leclaire, 'L'inconscient', in *Temps Modernes*, no. 183, July 1963, pp. 81 ff.

[49] E. Benveniste, 'Nature du signe linguistique', in *Acta linguistica*, I, 1939.

[50] A. Martinet, *Economie des changements phonétiques* (Francke, 1955), 5, 6.

[51] Cf. G. Mounin, 'Communication linguistique humaine et communication non-linguistique animale', in *Temps Modernes*, April–May 1960.

[52] Another example would be the Highway Code.

[53] Cf. *infra*, III.3.5.

[54] Saussure, *Cours de Linguistique Générale*, p. 115. *Course in General Linguistics*, tr. by W. Baskin (New York Library and Peter Owen, London, 1950), pp. 79–80.

[55] We may recall that since Saussure's day, History too has discovered the importance of synchronic strutures. Economics,

NOTES

linguistics, ethnology and history constitute today a *quad-rivium* of pilot sciences.

[56] Saussure, in R. Godel, op. cit., p. 90.

[57] Ibid., p. 166. It is obvious that Saussure was thinking of the comparison of the signs not on the plane of syntagmatic succession, but on that of the potential paradigmatic reserves, or associative fields.

[58] Saussure, *Cours de Linguistique Générale*, pp. 170 ff. *Course in General Linguistics*, pp. 122 ff.

[59] Paradeigma: model, table of the flexions of a word given as model, declension.

[60] R. Jakobson, 'Deux aspects du langage et deux types d'aphasie', in *Temps Modernes*, no. 188, Jan. 1962, pp. 853 ff., reprinted in *Essais de Linguistique générale* (Editions de Minuit, 1963), Ch. 2.

[61] This is only a very general polarization, for in fact metaphor and definition cannot be confused (cf. R. Jakobson, *Essais* ... , p. 220).

[62] Cf. R. Barthes, 'L'imagination du signe', in *Essais Critiques* (Seuil, 1964).

[63] 'Glottic': which belongs to the language – as opposed to speech.

[64] B. Mandelbrot has very rightly compared the evolution of linguistics to that of the theory of gases, *from the standpoint of discontinuity* ('Linguistique statistique macroscopique', in *Logique, Langage et Théorie de l'Information* (P.U.F., 1957)).

[65] L. Hjelmslev, *Essais linguistiques*, p. 103.

[66] *Langage des machines et langage humain*, Hermann, 1956, p. 91.

[67] In principle, for we must set aside the case of the distinctive units of the second articulation, cf. *infra*, same paragraph.

[68] Cf. *supra*, II.1.2.

[69] The problem of the syntagmatic segmentation of the significant units has been tackled in a new fashion by A. Martinet in the fourth chapter of his *Elements* ...

[70] Cf. *supra*, II.1.4.

[71] This may prove to be the case with all signs of connotation (cf. *infra*, Ch. IV).

[72] Broadly speaking, an exclamation (*oh*) may seem to be a syntagm made of a single unit, but in fact speech must here be restored to its context: the exclamation is an answer to a 'silent' syntagm. Cf. K. L. Pike: *Language in Relation to a*

Unified Theory of the Structure of Human Behaviour (Glendale, 1951).

[13] Saussure, quoted by R. Godel, *Les sources manuscrites du Cours de Linguistique Générale de F. de Saussure* (Droz-Minard, 1957), p. 90.

[14] A. Martinet, *Economie des changements phonétiques* (Francke, Berne, 1955), p. 22.

[15] Saussure, quoted by Godel, op. cit., p. 55.

[16] Ibid., p. 196.

[17] Cf. Frei's analysis of the sub-phonemes, *supra*, II.1.2.

[18] The phenomenon appears clearly at the level of a (monolingual) dictionary: the dictionary seems to give a positive definition of a word; but as this definition is itself made up of words which must themselves be explained, the positivity is endlessly referred further. Cf. J. Laplanche and S. Leclaire, 'L'inconscient', in *Temps Modernes*, no. 183, July 1961.

[19] *Cahiers Ferdinand de Saussure*, IX, pp. 11–40.

[80] All the oppositions suggested by Cantineau are binary.

[81] This is also a privative opposition.

[82] The economics of linguistics teaches us that there is a constant proportion beween the quantity of information to be transmitted and the energy (the time) which is necessary for this transmission (A. Martinet, *Travaux de l'Institut de Linguistique*, I, p. 11).

[83] Saussure, *Cours de linguistique générale*, p. 124.

[84] H. Frei, *Cahiers Ferdinand de Saussure*, XI, p. 35.

[85] *Destouches*, Logistique, p. 73.

[86] Cl. Lévi-Strauss, 'Introduction à l'œuvre de M. Mauss', in M. Mauss, *Sociologie et Anthropologie* (P.U.F., 1950), L, note.

[87] Cf. *Writing Degree Zero*.

[88] In *stallion/mare*, the common element is on the plane of the signified.

[89] Cantineau has not kept the *gradual oppositions*, postulated by Trubetzkoy (in German: *u/o* and *ü/ö*).

[90] Cf. R. Barthes, *Système de la Mode*, Seuil (1967).

[91] We shall not touch here on the question of the order of the terms in a paradigm; for Saussure, this order is indifferent; for Jakobson, on the contrary, in a flexion, the nominative or zero-case is the initial case (*Essais . . .*, p. 71, 'Typological studies and their contribution to historical comparative linguistics', in *Proceedings of the VIIIth International Congress of Linguists*, 1957 (Oslo), pp. 17–25, Chapter III of *Essais de Linguistique Générale*). This question can become very important on the day when the metaphor, for instance, is

studied as a paradigm of signifiers, and when it has to be decided whether one term in the series has some sort of precedence. Cf. R. Barthes, 'La Métaphore de l'œil', in *Critique*, nos. 195–6, August–September 1963, and *Essais Critiques* (Seuil, 1954).

[92] *Cours de Linguistique générale*, p. 174. Course in General Linguistics, p. 126.

[93] *Preliminaries to Speech Analysis* (Cambridge, Mass.), 1952.

[94] *Économie des changements phonétiques*, 3, 15, p. 73.

[95] More rudimentary senses, like smell and taste, however, seem to be 'analogical'. Cf. V. Bélévitch, *Langage des machines et langage humain*, pp. 74–5.

[96] *Cahiers de Lexicologie*, I, 1959 ('Unité sémantique complexe et neutralisation').

[97] It is of course the *discourse* of the fashion magazine which carries out the neutralization; the latter consists, in fact, in passing from the exclusive disjunction of the AUT type (chandail *or alternatively* sweater) to the inclusive disjunction of the VEL type (chandail or sweater *indifferently*).

[98] *Cahiers Ferdinand de Saussure*, IX, pp. 41–6.

[99] Cf. J. Laplanche et S. Leclaire, art. cit.

[100] Cf. R. Barthes, 'L'activité structuraliste', in *Essais Critiques* (Seuil, 1964), p. 213.

[101] Formulated by A. Martinet, *Élements . . .*, p. 37. *Elements of General Linguistics*, p. 40.

BIBLIOGRAPHY

Semiology cannot at the present time produce an autonomous bibliography; the main books must necessarily bear upon the work of linguists, ethnologists and sociologists who refer back to structuralism or the semantic model. We present here a limited selection of works (taken from the Gonthier edition of this book) which provide a good introduction to semiological analysis.

ALLARD, M., ELZIÈRE, M., GARDIN, J. C., HOURS, F., *Analyse conceptuelle du Coran sur cartes perforées*, Paris, La Haye, Mouton & Co., 1963, Vol. I, Code, 110 pp., Vol II, Commentary, 187 pp.

BARTHES, R., *Mythologies*, Paris, ed. du Seuil, 1957, 270 pp.

BRØNDAL, V., *Essais de Linguistique générale*, Copenhagen, 1943, Munksgaard, XII, 172 pp.

BUYSSENS, E., *Les Langages et le discours, Essai de linguistique fonctionnelle dans le cadre de la sémiologie*, Brussels, 1943, Office de Publicité, 97 pp.

ERLICH, V., *Russian Formalism*, Mouton & Co., s'Gravenhage, 1955, XIV, 276 pp.

GODEL, R., *Les sources manuscrites du Cours de Linguistique générale de F. de Saussure*, Geneva, Droz, Paris, Minard, 1957, 283 pp.

GRANGER, G. G., *Pensée formelle et sciences de l'homme*, Paris, Aubier, ed. Montaigne, 1960, 226 pp.

HARRIS, Z. S., *Methods in Structural Linguistics*, University of Chicago Press, Chicago, 1951, XV, 384 pp.

HJELMSLEV, L., *Essais Linguistiques*, Travaux du Cercle Linguistique de Copenhague, vol. XIII,

Copenhagen, Nordisk Sprog- og Kulturforlag. 1959, 276 pp.

JAKOBSON, R., *Essais de Linguistique Générale*, éd. de Minuit, Paris, 1963, 262 pp.
The full title of each essay quoted is given in the notes.

LEVI-STRAUSS, C., *Anthropologie Structurale*, Paris, Plon, 1958, II, 454 pp. *Structural Anthropology*, translated by Claire Jacobson and Brooke Grundfest Schoepf, Basic Books, New York and London, 1963, 410 pp.

MARTINET, A., *Éléments de Linguistique Générale*, Paris, A. Colin, 1960, 224 pp. *Elements of General Linguistics*, translated by Elisabeth Palmer, Faber & Faber, 1964, 205 pp.

MOUNIN, G., *Les Problèmes théoriques de la traduction*, Paris, Gallimard, 1963, XII, 301 pp.

MORRIS., C. W., *Signs, Language and Behaviour*, New York, Prentice-Hall Inc., 1946, XIII, 365 pp.

PEIRCE, C. S., *Selected Writings*, ed. by J. Buchlev, Harcourt, Bruce & Co., New York, London, 1940.

PIKE, K. L., *Language in Relation to a Unified Theory of the Structure of Human Behavior*, Glendale, Calif., 3 fasc. 1954, 1955, 1960, 170–85–146 pp.

PROPP, V., 'Morphology of the Folktale,' *Intern. Journal of American Linguistics*, vol. 24; no. 4, Oct. 1958, Indiana University, X, 134 pp.

SAUSSURE, F. de, *Cours de Linguistique Générale*, Paris, Payot, 4th edition, 1949, 331 pp. *Course of General Linguistics*, transl. W. Baskin, New York Library, and Peter Owen, London, 1960.

TRUBETZKOY, N. S., *Principes de Phonologie*, translated by J. Cantineau, Klincksiek, Paris, 1957, 1st edition, 1949, XXXIV, 396 pp.

BIBLIOGRAPHY

For recent developments in structural linguistics, the reader is referred to N. Ruwet's important article: 'La Linguistique générale aujourd'hui', in *Arch. europ. de Soc.*, V (1964), pp. 277–310.

A much fuller 'Bibliographie critique', covering all the aspects dealt with by all the studies contained in *Communications* No. 4, can be found in that periodical. *Communications* No. 8, which is devoted to 'The Structural Analysis of the Narrative', also contains a 'Bibliographie critique'.

INDEX

INDEX

INDEX

SELECTED BIBLIOGRAPHY

A list of the principal works of Roland Barthes, with the
date of their first appearance

LE DEGRÉ ZÉRO DE L'ÉCRITURE
  (Seuil, 1953)

MICHELET PAR LUI-MÊME
  (Collection: *Écrivains de Toujours*, no. 19, Seuil,
  1954)

MYTHOLOGIES
  (Seuil, 1957)

SUR RACINE
  (Seuil, 1963)

ESSAIS CRITIQUES
  (Seuil, 1964)

'ÉLÉMENTS DE SÉMIOLOGIE'
  (*Communications*, no. 4, Seuil, 1964)

CRITIQUE ET VÉRITÉ
  (Seuil, 1966)

THE AUTHOR

Roland Barthes was born in 1915 and studied French literature and Classics at the University of Paris. In 1936 he founded at the Sorbonne the Groupe Théâtral Antique. After a long illness, he taught French at universities in Rumania and Egypt, after which he joined the Centre National de la Recherche Scientifique, devoting himself to research in sociology and lexicology. In 1947 Barthes published a number of articles on literary criticism and the nature of writing in *Combat*, a Paris newspaper then run by Maurice Nadeau. These became eventually *Le Degré Zéro de L'Écriture*, which launched his career as a critic. He took part in founding the magazine *Théâtre Populaire* and has been one of the main advocates of the Brechtian cause in France, besides being one of the principal commentators on the theories of Robbe-Grillet and the *nouveau roman*. A controversy about criticism which has brought him into conflict with Professor Raymond Picard has of late made him a key figure in French literary debates.

Roland Barthes is now Directeur d'Études in the VIth section of the École Pratique des Hautes Études where he teaches a course on the sociology of signs, symbols and collective representations.